Microsoft® Word 2002

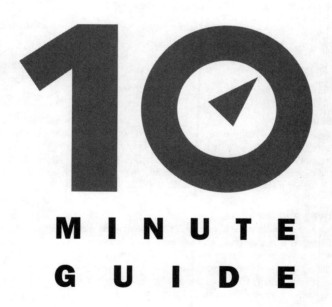

10

MINUTE
GUIDE

201 West 103rd Street
Indianapolis, IN 46290

Joe Habraken

10 Minute Guide to Microsoft® Word 2002

Copyright © 2002 by Que® Corporation

International Standard Book Number: 0-7897-2636-x

Library of Congress Catalog Card Number: 20-01090295

Printed in the United States of America

First Printing: August 2001

04   03   02   8   7   6

Trademarks

Warning and Disclaimer

Associate Publisher
Greg Wiegand

Managing Editor
Thomas Hayes

Acquisitions Editor
Stephanie J. McComb

Development Editor
Stephanie J. McComb

Project Editor
Tricia Liebig

Indexer
Sheila Schroeder

Proofreader
Amy Jay

Team Coordinator
Sharry Lee Gregory

Interior Designer
Gary Adair

Cover Designer
Alan Clements

Page Layout
Susan Geiselman

Contents

DEDICATION

To my nieces, Ryland and Lena.

ACKNOWLEDGMENTS

Creating books like this takes a real team effort. I would like to thank Stephanie McComb, our acquisitions editor, who worked very hard to assemble the team that made this book a reality and also served as the development editor for this book—coming up with many great ideas for improving the content of the book. Also, a great big thanks to our project editor, Tricia Liebig, who ran the last leg of the race and made sure the book made it to press on time—what a great team of professionals.

TELL US WHAT YOU THINK!

As the reader of this book, *you* are our most important critic and commentator. We value your opinion and want to know what we're doing right, what we could do better, what areas you'd like to see us publish in, and any other words of wisdom you're willing to pass our way.

As an Associate Publisher for Que, I welcome your comments. You can fax, e-mail, or write me directly to let me know what you did or didn't like about this book—as well as what we can do to make our books stronger.

Please note that I cannot help you with technical problems related to the topic of this book, and that due to the high volume of mail I receive, I might not be able to reply to every message.

When you write, please be sure to include this book's title and author as well as your name and phone or fax number. I will carefully review your comments and share them with the author and editors who worked on the book.

Fax: 317-581-4666

E-mail: feedback@quepublishing.com

Mail: Greg Wiegand
              Que
              201 West 103rd Street
              Indianapolis, IN 46290 USA

Introduction

Microsoft Word 2002 is an incredibly versatile and easy-to-use word processing program that can help you create business and personal documents. You can create simple documents, such as memos and outlines, and complex documents, such as newsletters and Internet-ready Web pages.

THE WHAT AND WHY OF MICROSOFT WORD

Word provides you with all the tools you need to quickly create many different types of word processing documents. Whether you work at home or in a busy office, Microsoft Word can provide you with the ability to do any of the following:

- Create memos and letters
- Build complex documents like brochures, reports, and even legal pleadings
- Use clipart, pictures, borders, and colors to add interest to your documents
- Create your own Web pages and Web site using the different Web Wizards

Additionally, Word provides a number of features that make it easy for you to create great looking documents whether you are working on a simple memo or a complex Web page. You can

- Quickly format text using Word Styles.
- Use the Autoformat feature to quickly format an entire document.
- Use sections in large documents to provide formatting for different document parts.
- Use the new speech feature for voice dictation and voice commands.

While providing you with many complex features, Microsoft Word is easy to learn. This book will help you understand the possibilities awaiting you with Microsoft Word 2002.

WHY QUE'S *10 MINUTE GUIDE TO MICROSOFT WORD 2002*?

The 10 Minute Guide to Microsoft Word 2002 can save you precious time while you get to know the different features provided by Microsoft Word. Each lesson is designed to be completed in 10 minutes or less, so you'll be up to snuff on basic and advanced Word skills quickly.

Although you can jump around among lessons, starting at the beginning is a good plan. The bare-bones basics are covered first, and more advanced topics are covered later. If you need help installing Word, see the next section for instructions.

CONVENTIONS USED IN THIS BOOK

The *10 Minute Guide to Microsoft Word 2002* includes step-by-step instructions for performing specific tasks. To help you as you work through these steps and help you move through the lessons easily, additional information is included and identified by the following icons.

PLAIN ENGLISH

New or unfamiliar terms are defined to help you as you work through the various steps in the lesson.

TIP

Read these tips for ideas that cut corners and confusion.

CAUTION

This icon identifies areas where new users often run into trouble; these hints offer practical solutions to those problems.

LESSON 1

What's New in Word 2002?

In this lesson, you are introduced to Word's powerful word processing and desktop publishing features, and you learn what's new in Word 2002.

GETTING THE MOST OUT OF WORD 2002

Microsoft Word is an efficient and full-featured word processor that provides you with all the tools you need to produce a tremendous variety of document types—everything from simple documents, such as memos and outlines, to complex documents, such as newsletters and Internet-ready Web pages.

Word provides a number of features to help you create personal and business documents. These features range from document wizards to easy document formatting options such as styles and the AutoFormat feature. Some of the Word features that you will explore in this book are:

- Wizards: Wizards such as the Memo Wizard, Mailing Label Wizard, and Web Page Wizard make it easy for you to create complex documents in Word. A wizard walks you through the creation of a particular document type using a step-by-step process. Wizards are covered in Lesson 3, "Working with Documents."

PLAIN ENGLISH

Wizard A feature that guides you step by step through a particular process in Word, such as creating a new document.

- Styles: A style is a grouping of formatting attributes identified by a style name. Styles can contain character-formatting attributes such as bold, or a particular font size. Styles can also contain attributes, such as alignment information, indents, and line spacing. Styles are covered in Lesson 12, "Working with Styles."

PLAIN ENGLISH

> **Style**   A collection of formatting attributes that is identified by a style name. Styles can quickly be assigned to text in your documents rather than adding each attribute individually to the text.

- AutoFormat: No matter what type of document you create, you can have Word add formatting to all the text in the document, providing you with a unified and professional look for any document. AutoFormat is covered in Lesson 13, "Using AutoFormatting to Change Text Attributes."

Whether you are a new Word user or are familiar with previous versions of Word, Word 2002 provides the proper level of features and help for you to immediately begin the document creation process.

NEW FEATURES IN WORD 2002

Word 2002 embraces a number of features that were first introduced with the release of Word 2000. For example, Word 2002 uses the same adaptive menu and toolbar system found in Word 2000 that customizes the commands and icons listed based on the commands you use most frequently.

Word 2002 also builds on the features found in the previous version of Word. It offers a number of new features that make it easier for you to input information into your Word documents and perform tasks related to the use of graphics in your documents and features, such as the Word Mail Merge. New features in Word 2002 range from smart tags to voice dictation to new ways to quickly get help.

For example, you will find that it is even easier to get help in Word 2002 than in previous versions of Word. A new feature—the Ask a Question Box—has been added to the top left of the Word application window, making it easier for you to get help on a particular topic as you work in Word. The various ways to get help in Word are covered in Lesson 5, "Getting Help in Microsoft Word." Let's take a survey of some of the other new features that are provided by Word 2002.

INTRODUCING TASK PANES

One of the biggest changes to the Word environment (and all the Microsoft Office XP member applications such as Word 2002, Excel 2002, and PowerPoint 2002) is the introduction of the Office task pane. The task pane is a special pane that appears on the right side of the Word application window. It is used to provide access to a number of Word features that were formerly controlled using dialog boxes.

For example, when you work with styles to format text in your Word document, you will access the various styles available in your document and create new styles using the Styles and Formatting task pane, which is shown in Figure 1.1.

Other task panes that you will run across as you use Word are the Office Clipboard and the Clip Gallery. The Office Clipboard allows you to copy or cut multiple items from a Word document and then paste them into a new location in the current or a new document. The Clip Gallery provides you with the ability to insert clip art into your Word document. Task panes are discussed throughout this book as you explore the various Word features.

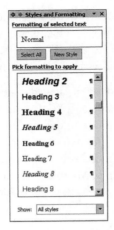

FIGURE 1.1
The Styles and Formatting task pane is used to manage and create styles for a Word document.

Smart Tags Provide Quick Options

Another new enhancement that Word 2002 provides is the smart tag. A smart tag is a special shortcut menu that provides you with additional options related to a particular feature. There are a number of smart tags including Paste smart tags and AutoCorrect smart tags.

For example, in cases where you cut or copy information from a Word document and paste it into a new location, you will find that a Paste smart tag appears at the bottom of the pasted item. This enables you to access options related to your paste job, such as whether the information pasted should maintain its original formatting or be formatted the same as text or numbers that are in the same part of the document where you pasted the new information. Figure 1.2 shows the smart tag that appears when an item is pasted in a Word document.

Smart tags are discussed throughout this book as you encounter them in relation to the various Word features.

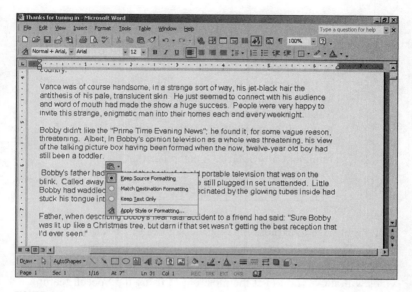

FIGURE 1.2
The Paste smart tag allows you to choose how the text is pasted into a Word document.

INTRODUCING VOICE DICTATION AND VOICE COMMANDS

Some of the most exciting new features in Word 2002 (and the entire Office XP suite) are voice dictation and voice-activated commands. If your computer is outfitted with a sound card, speakers, and a microphone (or a microphone with an earphone headset), you can dictate information into your Word documents. You also can use voice commands to activate the menu system in that application.

Before you can really take advantage of the Speech feature, you must provide it with some training so that it can more easily recognize your speech patterns and intonation. After the Speech feature is trained, you can effectively use it to dictate text entries or access various application commands without a keyboard or mouse.

CAUTION

> **Requirements for Getting the Most Out of the
> Speech Feature**   To make the Speech feature useful,
> you will need a fairly high-quality microphone. Microsoft
> suggests a microphone/headset combination. The
> Speech feature also requires a more powerful computer.
> Microsoft suggests using a computer with 128MB of
> RAM and a Pentium II (or later) processor running at a
> minimum of 400MHz. A computer that meets or
> exceeds these high standards should be capable of get-
> ting the most out of the Speech feature.

You might wish to explore the other lessons in this book, if you are
new to Word, before you attempt to use the Speech feature. Having a
good understanding of how Word operates and the features that it provides will allow you to get the most out of using the Speech feature.

TRAINING THE SPEECH FEATURE

The first time you start the Speech feature in Word, you are required
to configure and train the feature. Follow these steps to get the Speech
feature up and running:

1. In Word, select the **Tools** menu and select **Speech**. The
   Welcome to Office Speech Recognition dialog box appears.
   To begin setting up your microphone and training the Speech
   feature, click the **Next** button.

2. The first screen of the Microphone Wizard appears. It asks
   you to make sure that your microphone and speakers are connected to your computer. If you have a headset microphone,
   this screen shows you how to adjust the microphone for use.
   Click **Next** to continue.

3. The next wizard screen asks you to read a short text passage
   so that your microphone volume level can be adjusted (see
   Figure 1.3). When you have finished reading the text, click
   Next to continue.

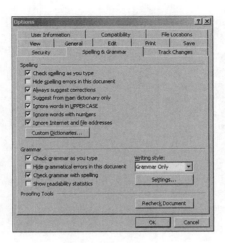

FIGURE 1.3
The Microphone Wizard adjusts the volume of your microphone.

4. On the next screen, you are told that if you have a headset microphone, you can click **Finish** and proceed to the speech recognition training. If you have a different type of microphone, you are asked to read another text passage. The text is then played back to you. This is to determine whether the microphone is placed at an appropriate distance from your mouth. When you get a satisfactory playback, click **Finish**.

When you finish working with the Microphone Wizard, the Voice Training Wizard appears. This wizard collects samples of your speech and educates the Speech feature as to how you speak.

To complete the voice training process, follow these steps:

1. After reading the information on the opening screen, click **Next** to begin the voice training process.

2. On the next screen, you are asked to provide your gender and age (see Figure 1.4). After specifying the correct information, click **Next**.

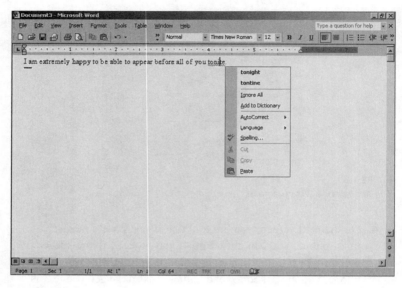

FIGURE 1.4
Supply the voice trainer with your gender and age.

3. On the next wizard screen, you are provided an overview of how the voice training will proceed. You are also provided with directions for how to pause the training session. Click **Next**.

4. The next wizard screen reminds you to adjust your microphone. You are also reminded that you need a quiet room when training the Speech feature. When you are ready to begin training the Speech Recognition feature, click **Next**.

5. On the next screen, you are asked to read text. As the wizard recognizes each word, the word is highlighted. After finishing with this screen, continue by clicking **Next**.

6. You are asked to read text on several subsequent screens. Words are selected as the wizard recognizes them.

7. When you complete the training screens, your profile is updated. Click **Finish** on the wizard's final screen.

You are now ready to use the Speech feature. The next two sections discuss using the Voice Dictation and Voice Command features.

CAUTION

> **The Speech Feature Works Better Over Time**   Be advised that the voice feature's performance improves as you use it. As you learn to pronounce your words more carefully, the Speech feature tunes itself to your speech patterns. You might need to do additional training sessions to fine-tune the Speech feature.

USING VOICE DICTATION

When you are ready to start dictating text into a Word document, put on your headset microphone or place your standalone microphone in the proper position that you determined when you used the Microphone Wizard. When you're ready to go, select the **Tools** menu and then select **Speech**. The Language bar appears, as shown in Figure 1.5. If necessary, click the **Dictation** button on the toolbar (if the Dictation button is not already activated or depressed).

After you enable the Dictation button, you can begin dictating your text into the Office document. Figure 1.5 shows text being dictated into a Word document. When you want to put a line break into the text, say "new line." Punctuation is placed in the document by saying the name of a particular punctuation mark, such as "period" or "comma."

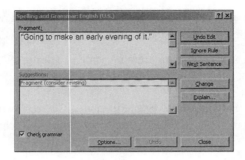

FIGURE 1.5
Dictating text into a Word document.

CAUTION

How Do I Insert the Word "Comma" Rather Than the Punctuation Mark?   Because certain keywords, such as "period" or "comma," are used to insert punctuation during dictation, you must spell these words out if you want to include them in the text. To do this, say "spelling mode," and then spell out the word, such as c-o-m-m-a. As soon as you dictate an entire word, the spelling mode is ended.

When you have finished dictating into the document, click the **Microphone** button on the Language bar (the second Microphone button from the left; the first is used to select the current speech driver, which you can leave as the default). When you click the **Microphone** button, the Language bar collapses and hides the Dictation and the Voice Command buttons. You can also stop Dictation mode by saying "microphone."

You can minimize the Language bar by clicking the **Minimize** button on the right end of the bar. This sends the Language bar to the Windows System Tray (it appears as a small square icon marked EN, if you are using the English version of Office).

With the Language bar minimized in the System Tray, you can quickly open it when you need it. Click the **Language Bar** icon in the

System Tray, and then select **Show the Language Bar** (which is the only choice provided when you click on the Language Bar icon).

Correctly using the Dictation feature requires you to know how to make the Speech feature place the correct text or characters into a Word document. For more help with the Dictation feature, consult the Microsoft Word Help system (discussed in Lesson 5).

USING VOICE COMMANDS

Another tool the Speech feature provides is voice commands. You can open and select menus in an application and even navigate dialog boxes using voice commands.

To use voice commands, open the Language bar (click **Tools**, **Speech**). Click the **Microphone** icon, if necessary, to expand the Language bar. Then, click the **Voice Command** icon on the bar (or say "voice command").

To open a particular menu such as the Format menu, say "format." Then, to open a particular submenu such as Font, say "font." In the case of these voice commands, the Font dialog box opens.

You can then navigate a particular dialog box using voice commands. You can also activate other font attributes in the dialog box in this manner. Say the name of the area of the dialog box you want to use, and then say the name of the feature you want to turn on or select.

When you have finished working with a particular dialog box, say "OK", and the dialog box closes and provides you with the features you selected in the dialog box. When you have finished using voice commands, say "microphone," or click the **Microphone** icon on the Language bar.

Believe it or not, you can also activate buttons on the various toolbars using voice commands!

In this lesson, you were introduced to Word 2002 and some of the new features available. In the next lesson, you will learn how to start Word and navigate the Word application window.

LESSON 2
Working in Word

In this lesson, you learn how to start Microsoft Word and navigate the Word window. You also learn how to use common tools such as menus, toolbars, and dialog boxes.

STARTING WORD

You create your documents in the Word window, which provides easy access to all the tools you need to create different types of Word documents including memos, letters, and even Web pages.

Before you can take advantage of Word's proficient document processing features, you must open the Word application window. To start the Word program, follow these steps:

1. From the Windows desktop, click **Start**, **Programs**. The Programs menu appears (see Figure 2.1).

2. To start Word, click the **Word** icon. The Word program window appears.

TIP

> **Create a Desktop Shortcut**   You can create a shortcut icon for Word on your desktop. Then, you can double-click this icon to start Word. Select the **Start** button, and point at **Programs**. Right-click the **Word** icon and select **Create Shortcut** from the menu that appears.

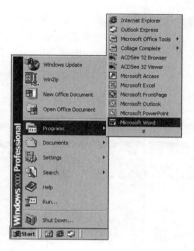

FIGURE 2.1
Open the Programs menu and click the Word icon to start Word.

Understanding the Word Environment

When you start the Word program, the Word application window
opens (see Figure 2.2). You create your documents in the Word window. The Word window also provides items that help you navigate and
operate the application itself.

TIP

> **Control the View** If your view differs from the view
> shown in Figure 2.2 (the Normal view), or if you don't
> see all the Word window elements shown in that figure
> (particularly the ruler), you can easily change your view.
> Select **View**, then choose the menu selection (such as
> **Normal** or **Ruler**) that matches your view to the figure.

Notice that the largest area of the window is blank; this is where you
create your new document. All the other areas—the menu bar, the
toolbar, and the status bar—either provide a fast way to access the

various commands and features that you use in Word, or they supply you with information concerning your document, such as what page you are on and where the insertion point is currently located in your document.

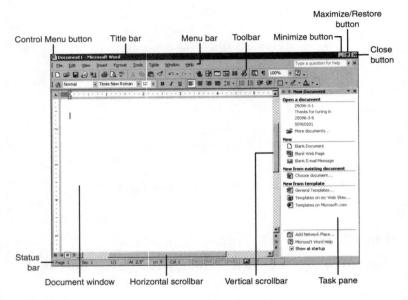

FIGURE 2.2
Create your documents and access Word's features and commands in the Word window.

Table 2.1 describes the elements you see in the Word application window.

TABLE 2.1   Elements of the Word Window

Element	Description
Title bar	Includes the name of the application and the current document, as well as the Minimize, Maximize, and Close buttons.

TABLE 2.1 (continued)

Element	Description
Control Menu button	Opens the Control menu, which provides such commands as Restore, Minimize, and Close.
Minimize button	Reduces the Word window to a button on the taskbar; to restore the window to its original size, click the button on the taskbar.
Maximize/Restore button	Enlarges the Word window to cover the Windows desktop. When the window is maximized, the Maximize button changes to a Restore button that you can click to return the window to its previous size.
Close (x) button	Closes the Word program. "x" is the icon for closing any window.
Menu bar	Contains menus of commands you can use to perform tasks in the program, such as Edit, Format, and Tools.
Toolbar	Includes icons that serve as shortcuts for common commands, such as Save, Print, and Spelling.
Status bar	Displays information about the current page number, the document section in which you are located, and the current location of the insertion point (inches, line, and column). The status bar also shows you other information, such as whether you have turned on the Typeover (OVR) mode by pressing the Insert key on the keyboard.
Document window	Where you type and format your documents.

TABLE 2.1   (continued)

Element	Description
Scrollbars	The horizontal scrollbar is used to scroll your view of the current document in a left-to-right motion. The vertical scrollbar is used to scroll up and down through the current document.
Task pane	The column of information on the right side of the document is the task pane. This is where you can access features such as the Clipboard, styles, and formatting; you can also open another document or mail merge.

USING MENUS AND TOOLBARS

Word provides several ways to access the commands and features you use as you create your documents. You can access these commands by using the menus on the menu bar and the buttons on the various toolbars.

You can also access many Word commands using shortcut menus. Right-clicking a particular document element (a word or a paragraph, for example) opens these menus, which contain a list of commands related to the item on which you are currently working.

THE WORD MENU BAR

The Word menu bar gives you access to all the commands and features that Word provides. Like all Windows applications, Word's menus reside below the title bar and are activated by clicking a particular menu choice. The menu then drops open, providing you with a set of command choices.

Word (and the other Office applications) adopted a menu system called personalized menus that enables you to quickly access the commands you use most often. When you first choose a particular menu, you find a short list of Word's most commonly used menu commands. This list of commands will actually be the ones that you have used most recently on that particular menu.

If a menu has a small double arrow at the bottom of its command list, you can click that to gain access to other, less commonly needed commands. As you use hidden commands, Word adds them to the normal menu list. This means that you are basically building the list of commands available on the menu as you use Word.

This personalized strategy is also employed by the toolbar system. As you use commands, they are added to the toolbar. However, this personalized toolbar feature is available only when you have the Standard toolbar and the Formatting toolbar on the same line in an application window. This provides you with customized menus and toolbars that are personalized for you.

To access a particular menu, follow these steps:

1. Select the menu by clicking its title (such as **View**), as shown in Figure 2.3. The most recently used commands appear; wait just a moment for all the commands on a particular menu to appear (if the commands do not appear, click the down arrow at the bottom of the menu).
2. Select the command on the menu that invokes a particular feature (such as **Header** and **Footer**).

You will find that many of the commands found on Word's menus are followed by an ellipsis (...). These commands, when selected, open a dialog box that requires you to provide Word with additional information before the particular feature or command can be used. More information about understanding dialog boxes is included later in this lesson.

FIGURE 2.3
Select a particular menu to view, and then point to a Word command.

Some of the menus also contain a submenu or cascading menu from which you make choices. The menu commands that produce a submenu are indicated by an arrow to the right of the menu choice. When a submenu is present, point at the command (marked with the arrow) on the main menu to open the submenu.

The menu system itself provides a logical grouping of the Word commands and features. For example, commands related to files, such as Open, Save, and Print, are all found on the File menu.

TIP

> **Activating Menus with the Keyboard**   You can activate a particular menu by holding down the **Alt** key and then pressing the keyboard key that matches the underscored letter in the menu's name. This underscored letter is called the hotkeyFor example, to activate the File menu in Word, press **Alt+F**.

If you find that you would rather have access to all the menu commands (rather than accessing only those you've used recently), you can turn off the personalized menu system. To do this, follow these steps:

1. Click the **Tools** menu, and then click **Customize**.

2. In the Customize dialog box, click the **Options** tab.

3. To show all the commands on the menus, click the **Always Show Full Menus** check box.

4. Click **OK** to close the dialog box.

SHORTCUT MENUS

A fast way to access commands related to a particular document element is to select that document object and then right-click. This opens a shortcut menu that contains commands related to the particular object with which you are working.

PLAIN ENGLISH

> **Object**   Any element found in a document, such as text, a graphic, a hyperlink, or other inserted item.

For example, if you select a line of text in a document, right-clicking the selected text (see Figure 2.4) opens a shortcut menu with commands such as Cut, Copy, and Paste, or it provides you with quick access to formatting commands, such as Font and Paragraph.

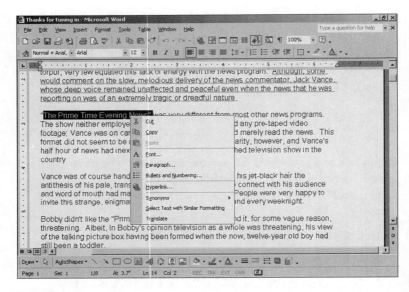

FIGURE 2.4
You can quickly access Word commands using shortcut menus.

WORD TOOLBARS

The Word toolbars provide a very quick and straightforward way to access commands and features. When you first start Word, you are provided with the Standard and Formatting toolbars, which reside as one continuous toolbar found directly below the menu bar.

To access a particular command using a toolbar button, click the button. Depending on the command, you see either an immediate result in your document (such as the removal of selected text when you click the **Cut** button) or the appearance of a dialog box requesting additional information from you.

TIP

> **Finding a Toolbar Button's Purpose**   You can hover (but do not click) the mouse pointer on any toolbar button to view a description of that tool's function.

Word offers several toolbars; many of them contain buttons for a specific group of tasks. For example, the Drawing toolbar provides buttons that give you access to tools that enable you to draw graphical elements in your documents (such as text boxes, lines, and rectangles).

To place additional toolbars in the Word window, right-click any toolbar currently shown and select from the list that appears. Specific toolbars exist for working with tables, pictures, and the World Wide Web.

You can also easily add or remove buttons from any of the toolbars present in the Word window. Each toolbar is equipped with a Toolbar Options button that you can use to modify the buttons shown on that particular toolbar.

To add or remove buttons from a toolbar, follow these steps:

1. Click the **Toolbar Options** button on any toolbar; a drop-down area appears.

2. Click **Add or Remove Buttons** and then select the name of the toolbar that appears on the pop-up menu. A list of all the buttons for the current toolbar appears, as shown in Figure 2.5.

3. For a button to appear on the toolbar, a check mark must appear to the left of the button in this list. For buttons without a check mark next to them, clicking this space puts the button on the toolbar. These buttons work as toggle switches; one click adds the check mark, another click removes it.

4. When you have completed your changes to the current toolbar, click outside the button list to close it.

The Word toolbars provide fast access to the commands you need most often. Buttons exist for all the commands that are available on the Word menu system.

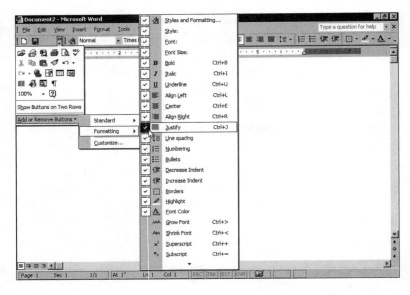

FIGURE 2.5
You can easily add or remove buttons from a toolbar using the button list.

TIP

> **Give the Standard Toolbar More Space**   Another way to provide more space for buttons on the toolbars is to place the Formatting toolbar below the Standard toolbar. Then, both toolbars have the width of the screen on which to display their respective buttons. Select the **Toolbar Options** button on a toolbar, and then select **Show Buttons on Two Rows**.

Exiting Word

When you have completed your initial survey of the Word application window or have completed your work in the program, exit the software. More than one way exists to close the Word window, which is the same as exiting the program.

You can exit Word by selecting the **File** menu and then **Exit**, or you can close Word with one click of the mouse by clicking the Word **Close (x)** button in the upper-right corner of the application window.

When you close Word, you might be prompted to save any work that you have done in the application window. If you were just experimenting as you read through this lesson, you can click **No**. The current document will not be saved, and the Word application window closes. All the ins and outs of saving your documents are covered in Lesson 3, "Working with Documents."

In this lesson, you learned how to start Word and explored the various parts of the Word window. You also learned how to work with the menu system, toolbars, and dialog boxes. Finally, you also learned how to exit the Word program. In the next lesson, you will learn how to create a new document and save your work.

LESSON 3
Working with Documents

In this lesson, you learn how to start a new document and enter text. You also learn how to take advantage of Word document templates and Word document wizards.

STARTING A NEW DOCUMENT

When you choose to start a new document in Word, you can take three routes. You can

- Create a blank new document using Word's default template.
- Create a document using one of Word's many other templates or a custom one you created yourself.
- Create a document using one of the Word *wizards*, such as the Fax or Envelope Wizard.

The amount of software assistance you get in creating your new document is greatly increased when you choose the template or wizard option.

PLAIN ENGLISH

Template A blueprint for a document that may already contain certain formatting options and text.

When you create a new document from scratch, you are actually using a template—the Blank Document template. Documents based on the Blank Document template do not contain any premade text (as some of the other templates do), and the formatting contained in the document reflects Word's default settings for margins, fonts, and other document attributes (including any you customized specifically to your needs or preferences). To find more information on default Word settings involving font and document attributes, see Lesson 7, "Changing How Text Looks," and Lesson 11, "Working with Margins, Pages, and Line Spacing," respectively).

As covered in Lesson 2, "Working in Word," Word automatically opens a new blank document for you when you start the Word software. You can also open a new document when you are already in the Word application window.

To open a new document, follow these steps:

1. Select **File**, and then **New**. The task pane opens on the right side of your screen. Under **New from Template**, select **General Templates** and Word opens the Templates dialog box with a range of templates from which to choose (see Figure 3.1).

2. Make sure that the General tab is selected in the Templates dialog box, and then double-click the Word **Blank Document** icon. A new document appears in the Word application window.

Although the steps shown here are designed for you to create a new blank document, you could have chosen any of the templates available in the Templates dialog box to create a new document. The fastest way to create a new blank document is to click the **New Blank Document** icon on the Word Standard toolbar.

CAUTION

What Happened to My Previous Document?   If you were already working on a document, the new document will, in effect, open on top of the document you were previously working on. You can get back to the previous document by clicking the appropriately named document icon on the Windows taskbar (if you haven't yet named the first document, it might appear as Document1 on the taskbar). You can also select the **Windows** menu to see a list of currently opened documents. Click any document in the list to switch to it.

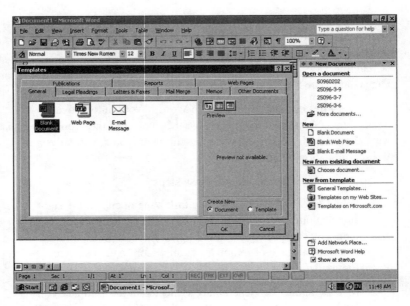

FIGURE 3.1
When you choose New on the File menu, the task pane opens and you can choose General Templates.

TIP

> **Removing Multiple Document Icons from the Taskbar**   If you prefer not to see the open document icons on the taskbar, select the **Tools** menu, select **Options**, and click the **View** tab. Clear the **Windows in Taskbar** check box. You must then use the Windows menu to switch between documents.

ENTERING TEXT

After you have opened a new document, you are ready to start entering text. Notice that a blinking vertical element called the *insertion point* appears in the upper-left corner of your new document. This is where new text will be entered.

Begin typing text from the keyboard. The insertion point moves to the right as you type. As soon as you reach the end of the line, the text automatically wraps to the next line if you are using word wrap.

When you reach the end of a paragraph in Word, you must press the **Enter** key to manually insert a line break. If you want to view the manually placed line breaks (called paragraph marks) in your document, click the **Show/Hide** button on the Word Standard toolbar.

If the Show/Hide button is not visible on the Word toolbar, click the **Tool Options** button located at the end of the Standard toolbar. From the shortcut menu that appears, select **Add or Remove Buttons** and then **Standard**. A drop-down box of other buttons, including the Show/Hide button, appears. Clicking this button adds it to the Standard toolbar. When you are finished, click outside the drop-down box to return to your document. Now you can turn the Show/Hide option on and off as previously described.

TIP

How Word Views Paragraphs   Word considers any line or series of lines followed by a line break (created when you press the Enter key) a separate paragraph. This concept becomes very important when you deal with paragraph formatting issues, such as line spacing, indents, and paragraph borders.

Using Document Templates

You don't have to base your new documents on a blank template. Instead, you can take advantage of one of the special document templates that Word provides. These templates make it easy for you to create everything from memos to newsletters.

Templates contain special text and document attributes; therefore, the look and layout of the document you create using a template are predetermined by the options contained in the template. This can include margins, fonts, graphics, and other document layout attributes.

To base a new document on a Word template, follow these steps:

1. Select the **File** menu, and then click **New**. The task pane opens in your current document window.

2. Several template category links are available under the **New from Template** heading. These links include categories such as Normal, General Templates, and Templates on Microsoft.com. Select the category link for the type of document you want to create. For example, to create a new memo, click the **General Templates** link. In the Templates dialog box that appears, choose the **Memos** tab (see Figure 3.2). Select your favorite style of memo and click **OK** (or double-click the icon of choice).

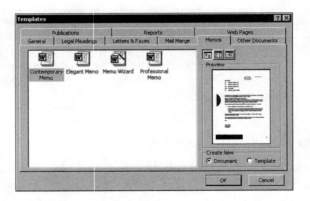

FIGURE 3.2
The document category tabs in the Templates dialog box contain templates for different document types.

3. The new document based on the template appears as shown in Figure 3.3.

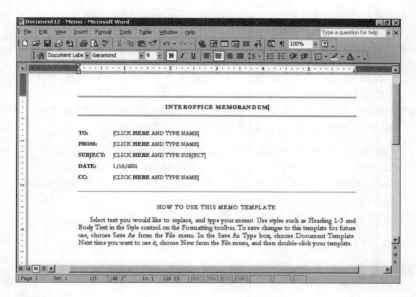

FIGURE 3.3
The new document contains predetermined text and formatting attributes derived from the template.

Most new documents based on templates already contain text, such as headings, as well as a variety of document layouts and text attributes, such as a particular font. For example, the document based on the Elegant Memo template already contains the layout for a memo, and it automatically enters the current date in the memo for you.

Text can easily be entered into the document using the Click Here and Type boxes that are placed in the document. Just click anywhere on the bracketed box and type the text you want to enter.

Many templates (the Elegant Memo template, for example) contain text that gives you advice on how to use the template. Any of this explanatory text can be selected and removed or replaced with your own text (for more about selecting text, see Lesson 4, "Editing Documents").

USING WORD WIZARDS

If you find that you would like even more help as you create a new document, you can use any of a number of Word document wizards. These wizards actually walk you through the document creation process, and in many cases, they make sure that you enter the appropriate text in the proper place in the new document.

The wizards are found on the same tabs that housed the templates located in the Templates dialog box (reached through the task pane). The wizards can be differentiated from standard templates by a small wizard's wand that appears over a template's icon.

To create a new document using one of the wizards, follow these steps:

1. Select the **File** menu, and then click **New** to open the task pane.

2. Under the **New from Template** heading, select the link for the document category you want to create (many useful templates are under the **General Templates** link). In the Templates dialog box that appears, choose the new document tab of your choice.

3. To start the document creation process using the wizard, double-click the appropriate wizard icon (for example, the Memo Wizard on the Memos tab).

When you double-click the wizard icon, the wizard dialog box opens with an introductory screen and outlines the document creation process for the type of document you want to create. For example, the Memo Wizard shown in Figure 3.4 details the memo creation process on the left side of the wizard dialog box.

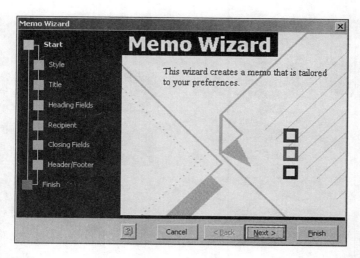

FIGURE 3.4

The various document wizards, such as the Memo Wizard, outline the new creation process and then walk you through the steps of creating the document.

If you find that you need help as you work with a wizard, you can click the **Office Assistant** button on the wizard dialog box. The Office Assistant, which appears as an animated paper clip by default, appears with context-sensitive help related to the wizard screen on which you are currently working. If the button is not available, cancel the wizard, select the **Help** menu, and then **Show the Office Assistant**; then repeat the steps necessary to open the particular document wizard.

To move to the next step in the document creation process, click the **Next** button at the bottom of the wizard screen.

The various document wizards walk you through the entire document creation process. After completing the steps for document creation, click the **Finish** button to close the wizard. A new document appears in the Word window based on the choices you made as you worked with the wizard. Figure 3.5 shows a new document created using the Memo Wizard.

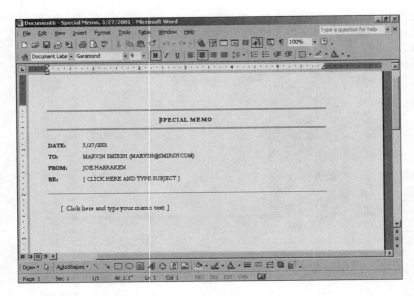

FIGURE 3.5
The Memo Wizard prompts you to input the appropriate information for a memo and provides the formatting for the new document.

The wizards you use vary in look and feel, depending on the type of document you are trying to create. For example, the Resume Wizard produces a decidedly different product than the Envelope Wizard does. A good rule to follow is to read each wizard screen carefully. Remember that you can always back up a step by clicking the **Back** button if you find that you've made an inappropriate choice (or you can close the unwanted document and start over).

SAVING A DOCUMENT

Whether you create your new document using the Blank Document template, a Word template, or a document wizard, at some point you will want to save the new document. Saving your work is one of the most important aspects of working with any software application. If you don't save your Word documents, you could lose them.

CAUTION

Save and Save Often   You don't want to lose your valuable documents as you create them in Word. Power failures, an accidentally kicked-out power cord, or your computer locking up as you work can all lead to lost work. If you are really absent-minded about periodically saving your work, use the AutoSave feature. Select the **Tools** menu, then **Options**. Click the **Save** tab on the dialog box. Make sure the **Save AutoRecover Info Every** check box is selected. Use the minutes box to set the time interval between autosaves. This feature doesn't replace periodically saving your document using the Save command, but it will help you recover more of your document if there is a problem such as a power failure.

To save a document, follow these steps:

1. Click the **Save** button on the Word toolbar, or select the **File** menu and then **Save**. The first time you save your new document, the Save As dialog box appears.

2. Type a filename into the File Name box. If you want to save the file in a format other than a Word document (.doc), such as a text file (.txt), click the **Save As Type** drop-down arrow and select a different file type.

3. To save the file to a different location (the default location is My Documents), click the **Save In** drop-down arrow. After you select a particular drive, all the folders on that drive appear.

4. Double-click the desired folder in the Save In box to open that folder.

5. After you have specified a name and a location for your new document, select the **Save** button to save the file. Word then returns you to the document window.

 As you edit and enhance your new document, you should make a habit of frequently saving any changes that you make. To save changes to a document that has already been saved under a filename, just click the **Save** button.

If you would like to keep a backup of a document (the version as it appeared the last time you saved it) each time you save changes to it, you need to set the backup option.

1. Click the **Tools** command on the toolbar, and then select **Options**.

2. In the Options dialog box, click the **Save** tab and then the **Always Create Backup Copy** check box. Click **OK** to return to the document.

3. Name your file and save it for the first time to an appropriate location.

Now, when you use the Save command to save changes you've made to the document, a backup copy of the file (with the extension.wbk) is also saved. This backup copy is the previous version of the document before you made the changes. Each subsequent saving of the document replaces the backup file with the previous version of the document.

There might be occasions when, rather than using the backup option, you want to save the current document under a new filename or drive location. This can be done using the Save As command. To save your document with a new filename, follow these steps:

1. Select **File**, and then **Save As**.

2. In the Save As dialog box, type the new filename into the File Name box (make sure that you are saving the document in the desired path).

3. Click **Save**. The file is saved under the new name.

Closing a Document

When you have finished working with a document, you need to save your changes and then close the document. To close a document, select the **File** menu and then select **Close**. You can also close a document by clicking the **Close (x)** button on the right side of the document window. If you are working with multiple documents, closing one of the documents does not close the Word application. If you want to completely end your Word session, select the **File** menu, and then select **Exit**. Before closing a document, Word checks to see whether it has changed since it was last saved. If it has, Word asks whether you want to save these changes before closing. If you don't want to lose any recent changes, click **Yes** to save the document.

Opening a Document

Opening an existing document is a straightforward process. You will find that the Open dialog box shares many of the attributes that you saw in the Save As dialog box.

To open an existing Word file, follow these steps:

1. Select the **File** menu, and then **Open**. The Open dialog box appears.

2. By default, Word begins showing the files and folders in your My Documents folder. If the document you need is located elsewhere on your computer, click the **Look In** drop-down arrow to select the drive on which the file is located, and navigate to the folder containing the document you need.

3. To open the file, click the file, and then click the **Open** button (you can also double-click the file). The file appears in a Word document window.

If you are working with text files or documents that have been saved in a format other than the Word document format (.doc), you must select the file type in the **Files of Type** drop-down box to see them.

In this lesson, you learned how to create a new blank document and base a new document on a Word template. You also learned how to create a new document using the Word wizards, how to open an existing document, and how to save your documents. In the next lesson, you will learn how to edit your document and delete, copy, and move text. You also will learn how to save your document under a new filename.

LESSON 4
Editing Documents

*In this lesson, you learn how to do basic text
editing in Word, including moving and copying text; you work with the
mouse and keyboard to move your document, and you learn how to
save existing documents under a new filename.*

ADDING OR REPLACING TEXT AND MOVING IN THE DOCUMENT

After you have completed a draft of your document, you probably will
find yourself in a situation where you want to add and delete text in
the document as you edit your work. Word makes it very easy for you
to add new text and delete text that you don't want. You also will find
that, whether you use the mouse or the keyboard to move around in
your document as you edit, Word offers a number of special key-
strokes and other tricks that make moving within the document a
breeze. Figure 4.1 highlights some of these tools and Word screen
areas.

ADDING NEW TEXT

You actually have two possibilities for adding text to the document:
insert and *typeover*. To insert text into the document and adjust the
position of the existing text, place the *I-beam* mouse pointer where
you want to insert the new text. Click the mouse to place the insertion
point at the chosen position. Make sure that the OVR indicator on the
Status bar is not active (it will be gray rather than bolded). This means
that you are in the insert mode.

I-beam: Used to place the
insertion point in the document.

Vertical scrollbar: Scroll up
and down in a document.

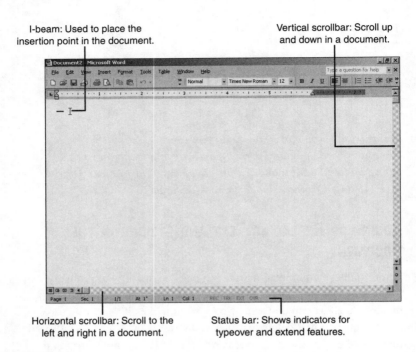

Horizontal scrollbar: Scroll to the
left and right in a document.

Status bar: Shows indicators for
typeover and extend features.

FIGURE 4.1
*A number of different tools and approaches are available for editing and select-
ing text in Word and moving around in your Word documents.*

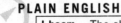

PLAIN ENGLISH

I-beam   The shape that the mouse pointer takes when
you place it over any text in a Word document. Use it to
place the insertion point at a particular position in a
document.

PLAIN ENGLISH

Insert Mode   The default text mode in Word. New text is
added at the insertion point and existing text is pushed
forward in the document so that it remains as part of
the document.

Type your new text. It is added at the insertion point, and existing text (the text to the right of the inserted text) is pushed forward in the document.

REPLACING TEXT

If you want to add new text to a document and simultaneously delete text to the right of the insertion point, use the mouse to place the insertion point where you want to start typing over the existing text. Press the **Insert** key on the keyboard and add your new text. The added text types over the existing text, deleting it (see Figure 4.2). When you switch to Typeover mode using the **Insert** key, the Word status bar displays the message OVR. This means that you are currently in Typeover mode.

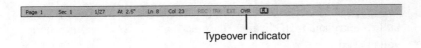

Typeover indicator

FIGURE 4.2
When you are in Typeover mode, existing text is overwritten by the new text.

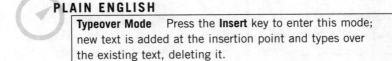

PLAIN ENGLISH

Typeover Mode   Press the **Insert** key to enter this mode; new text is added at the insertion point and types over the existing text, deleting it.

If you want to return to Insert mode, press the **Insert** key again (it toggles Word between the Insert and Typeover modes) and the OVR message on the status bar is dimmed (you can also double-click **OVR** on the status bar to toggle this feature on and off).

CAUTION

> **Undo That Typeover**   If you inadvertently type over text in a document because you are in the Typeover mode, click the **Undo** button (it might take several clicks in cases where you have added several words to the document) on the toolbar to return the deleted text to the document (or press **Ctrl+Z**).

MOVING AROUND THE DOCUMENT

Whether you are a mouse aficionado or prefer to stick close to your keyboard, Word provides several shortcuts and tools for moving around a document that you are trying to edit.

When you use the mouse, you can move to a different position in the current page by placing the mouse pointer (the I-beam) over a particular text entry and then clicking. This places the insertion point where you clicked.

You also can use the mouse to move through your document using the vertical and horizontal scrollbars. For example, clicking the up-scroll arrow on the vertical scrollbar moves you up through the document. Clicking the down-scroll arrow moves you down through the document. If you want to quickly move to a particular page in the document, you can drag the scroll box to a particular place on the vertical scrollbar. As soon as you click the scrollbox, a page indicator box appears that you can use to keep track of what page you are on as you drag the scroll box up or down on the vertical scrollbar.

The vertical scrollbar also provides Previous Page and Next Page buttons (the double-up arrow and double-down arrow buttons on the bottom of the scrollbar) that can be used to move to the previous page and next page, respectively. Use the mouse to click the appropriate button to move in the direction that you want to go in your document.

The horizontal scrollbar operates much the same as the vertical scrollbar; however, it offers the capability to scroll only to the left and the right of a document page. This is particularly useful when you have zoomed in on a document and want to scrutinize an area of the page in great detail.

You should be aware that clicking the mouse on the vertical scrollbar to change your position in a document allows you to view a different portion of a page or a different part of the document; however, it does not move the insertion point to that position on the page. To actually place the insertion point, you must move to a specific place or position in the document, and then click the mouse I-beam where you want to place the insertion point.

When you're typing or editing text, you might find that the fastest way to move through the document is with the help of the keyboard shortcuts shown in Table 4.1. Keeping your hands on the keyboard, rather than reaching out for the mouse, can be a more efficient way to move in a document while you compose or edit.

 TIP

> **Scroll Quickly with a Wheel Mouse**   You might want to purchase a wheel mouse, such as Microsoft's IntelliMouse, which provides a rolling device on the top of mouse (between the click buttons). With your finger on the wheel device, you can literally "roll" the vertical scrollbar through the document at the pace of your choice—rapidly or slowly.

TABLE 4.1   Using the Keyboard to Move Through the Document

Key Combination	Movement
Home	Move to the beginning of a line
End	Move to the end of a line
Ctrl+Right arrow	Move one word to the right

TABLE 4.1   (continued)

Key Combination	Movement
Ctrl+Left arrow	Move one word to the left
Ctrl+Up arrow	Move to the previous paragraph
Ctrl+Down arrow	Move to the next paragraph
PgUp	Move up one window
PgDn	Move down one window
Ctrl+PgUp	Move up one page
Ctrl+PgDn	Move down one page
Ctrl+Home	Move to the top of a document
Ctrl+End	Move to the bottom of a document

SELECTING TEXT

Having a good handle on the different methods for selecting text in a document makes it easy for you to take advantage of many features, including deleting, moving, and formatting text. You can select text with either the mouse or the keyboard. Both methods have their own advantages and disadvantages as you work on your documents.

SELECTING TEXT WITH THE MOUSE

The mouse is an excellent tool for selecting text in your document during the editing process. You can double-click a word to select it and also use different numbers of mouse clicks (quickly pressing the left mouse button) or the mouse in combination with the Shift key to select sentences, paragraphs, or other blocks of text. You also can hold the left mouse button down and drag it across a block of text that you want to select.

How you use the mouse to select the text depends on whether the mouse pointer is in the document itself or along the left side of the document in the *selection bar*. The selection bar is the whitespace on the left edge of your document window, just in front of your text paragraphs. When you place the mouse in the selection bar, the mouse pointer becomes an arrow (in contrast to placing the mouse in the document where the pointer appears as an I-beam).

Selecting text lines and paragraphs from the selection bar makes it easy for you to quickly select either a single line or the entire document. Table 4.2 shows you how to select different text items using the mouse. Figure 4.3 shows the mouse pointer in the selection bar with a selected sentence.

TABLE 4.2   Using the Mouse to Quickly Select Text in the Document

Text Selection	Mouse Action
Selects the word	Double-click a word
Selects text block	Click and drag
	Or
	Click at beginning of text, and then hold down Shift key and click at the end of text block
Selects line	Click in selection bar next to line
Selects multiple lines	Click in selection bar and drag down through multiple lines
Selects the sentence	Hold Ctrl and click a sentence
Selects paragraph	Double-click in selection bar next to paragraph
	Or
	Triple-click in the paragraph
Selects entire document	Hold down Ctrl and click in selection bar

You will find these mouse manipulations are particularly useful when you are editing the document. Selected text can be quickly deleted, moved, or copied.

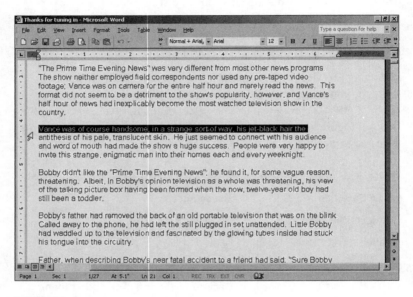

FIGURE 4.3
Place the mouse pointer in the selection bar to quickly select a line, a para-graph, or other text block.

SELECTING TEXT WITH THE KEYBOARD

You can also select text using only the keyboard. Press the **F8** function key to turn on the extend (or select) feature; the EXT indicator becomes active on the Word status bar (meaning it is no longer "grayed" out).

To select text using the extend feature, use the arrow keys to move over and highlight characters, words, or sentences you want to select. You can quickly select entire words by pressing **F8** and then pressing the spacebar. To select an entire sentence, turn on the extend feature, and then press the period (.) key. Entire paragraphs can be selected using this method by pressing the **Enter** key. To turn off the extend feature, press the **Esc** key.

Finally, you can select text by pressing only the F8 function key. Press **F8** once to turn on the select feature where you want it, press it twice to select a word, three times to highlight an entire sentence, four times to select a paragraph, and five times to select your entire document.

DELETING, COPYING, AND MOVING TEXT

Another important aspect of editing is being able to delete, move, or copy text in your document. Each of these tasks can be easily accomplished in Word and uses the mouse or the keyboard to select the text that you want to delete, move, or copy. Then, it's just a matter of invoking the correct command to delete, move, or copy the selected text.

DELETING TEXT

Deleting text can be accomplished in more than one way. The simplest way to remove characters as you type is with the Backspace key or the Delete key. With no selected text

- **Delete**—Deletes the character to the right of the insertion point.

- **Backspace**—Deletes the character to the left of the insertion point.

You will probably find, however, that when you delete text you want to remove more than just one character, so use the keyboard or the mouse to select the text you want to delete. After the text is selected, press the **Delete** key. The text is then removed from the document.

You can also delete text and replace it with new text in one step. After the text is selected, type the new text. It replaces the entire existing, selected text.

CAUTION

> **Delete and Cut Are Different**   When you want to erase a
> text block forever, use the **Delete** key. When you want to
> remove text from a particular place in the document but
> want to have access to it again to place it somewhere
> else, use the **Cut** command on the **Edit** menu. When you
> cut an item, it is automatically placed on the Office
> Clipboard. These steps are covered later in this lesson.

COPYING, CUTTING, AND PASTING TEXT

Copying or cutting text and then pasting the copied or cut item to a
new location is very straightforward. All you have to do is select the
text as we have discussed earlier in this lesson and then invoke the
appropriate commands. Use the following steps to copy and paste text
in your document:

1. Using the mouse or the keyboard, select the text that you
   want to copy.

2. Select the **Edit** menu and then select **Copy**, or press **Ctrl+C**
   to copy the text.

3. Place the insertion point in the document where you want to
   place a copy of the copied text.

4. Select the **Edit** menu and then select **Paste**, or press **Ctrl+V**.
   A copy of the text is inserted at the insertion point.

TIP

> **Use the Copy, Cut, and Paste Icons**   To
> quickly access the copy, cut, and paste features, use
> the Copy, Cut, and Paste icons on the Word toolbar,
> respectively.

After pasting your selected text, the Paste smart tag icon appears just below the text that you have pasted. When you click this icon, it provides a shortcut menu that allows you to keep the formatting that was applied to the source text that you copied, match the formatting supplied by the destination for the text (the paragraph in which the text is placed), or just paste the text into the new location with no formatting at all (which means it will assume the formatting that is provided at the current location).

Smart tags are a new feature found in Word 2002. Figure 4.4 shows pasted text and the Paste smart tag provided for the text.

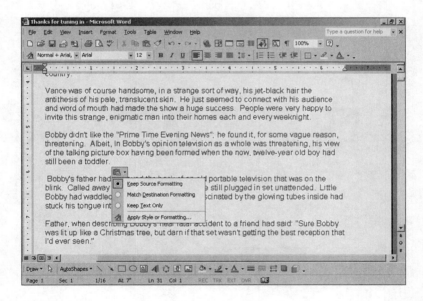

FIGURE 4.4
The Paste smart tag allows you to choose how the text is pasted into the new location.

Cutting text from the document and then pasting it to a new location is every bit as straightforward as using copy and paste. Select the text, and then press **Ctrl+X** or click the **Cut** button on the Standard toolbar. Click the I-beam to place the insertion point on the document, and then you can then use **Ctrl+V** or the **Paste** button on the Standard toolbar to place the text in a new location. A Paste smart tag will appear below the pasted text as shown in Figure 4.4.

Using the Office Clipboard to Copy and Move Multiple Items

The Office Clipboard feature now resides in the task pane of your Office application windows. If you want to copy or cut more than one item and then be able to paste them into different places in the document, you must use the Office Clipboard. Follow these steps:

1. To open the Clipboard task pane, select the **Edit** menu and select **Office Clipboard**. The Clipboard appears in the task pane.

2. As shown in Figure 4.5, select and copy each item to the Clipboard.

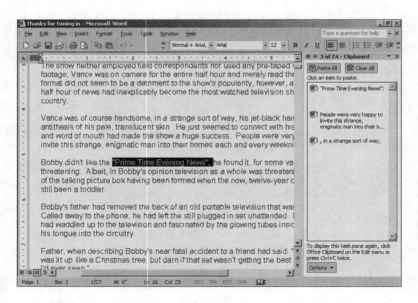

FIGURE 4.5
The Clipboard can hold up to 24 separate items.

3. After you have copied your items onto the Clipboard, place the insertion point where you want the first item to be pasted. Then, return to the Clipboard and with the mouse, point to your first item and click; Word automatically inserts the item into the document.

4. Repeat step 3 as needed to paste other items from the Clipboard into your document.

If you want to cut and paste (or move) multiple items, you must use the Office Clipboard. Follow these steps:

1. To open the Clipboard, select the **Edit** menu and select **Clipboard**. The Clipboard appears in the task pane.

2. Select and cut each item to the Clipboard.

3. After you have your cut items on the Clipboard, place the insertion point where you want the first item to be pasted. Then, return to the Clipboard and with the mouse, point to your first item and click; it will automatically be inserted into the document.

4. Repeat step 3 as needed to paste other items from the Clipboard into your document.

USING DRAG AND DROP

One other way to move text is by selecting it and dragging it to a new location. This is called drag and drop. After the text is selected, place the mouse on the text block and hold down the left mouse button. A Move pointer appears, as shown in Figure 4.6.

Drag the Move pointer to the new location for the text. A dotted insertion point appears in the text. Place this insertion point in the appropriate position and release the mouse button. The text is moved to the new location.

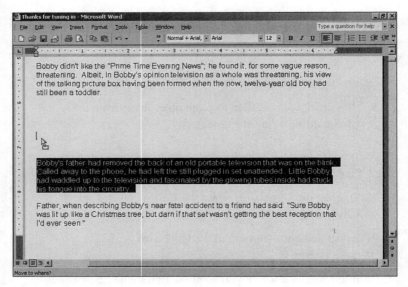

FIGURE 4.6
Drag a block of selected text to a new location with drag and drop.

COPYING AND MOVING TEXT BETWEEN DOCUMENTS

You can copy and move text easily between documents. All you have to do is open the appropriate documents and then use the methods already discussed for copying or moving text. You can even use drag and drop to move information from one document to another.

To copy information from one document to another, follow these steps:

1. Open the document you want to copy information from and the one you want to copy that information to (see Lesson 3, "Working with Documents," for more information on opening documents).

2. Switch to the document that contains the text you want to copy by clicking the document's button on the **Taskbar** or selecting the **Windows** menu and then the name of the document.

3. Select the text you want to copy, select the **Edit** menu, and then select the **Copy** command.

4. Using the instructions in step 3, switch to the document into which you want to paste the text.

5. Select the **Edit** menu and then select **Paste**. The text is pasted into your document.

You can also use the preceding steps to move text from one document to another by substituting the Cut command for the Copy command. You can also use drag and drop to move text from one document to another. Working with multiple document windows can be tricky. You probably won't want to have more than two documents open at a time if you want to use drag and drop. (There won't be enough space in the Word workspace to scroll through the documents and find the text you want to move or the final resting place for the text in the other document.)

To view multiple document windows, open the desired documents. Select the **Windows** menu and then select **Arrange All**. Each document is placed in a separate window in the Word workspace. The windows might be small if you have several documents open. Locate the text you want to move and select it. Drag it from the current document window to the document window and position where you want to place it.

In this lesson, you learned basic editing techniques including the deleting, copying, and moving of text. You also learned to move around your documents and various ways to select text. You also worked with multiple documents and copied text from one document to another. In the next lesson you will learn how to get help in Word.

LESSON 5

Getting Help in Microsoft Word

In this lesson, you learn how to access and use the Help system in Microsoft Word.

HELP: WHAT'S AVAILABLE?

Microsoft Word supplies a Help system that makes it easy for you to look up information on Word commands and features as you work on your documents. Because every person is different, the Help system can be accessed in several ways. You can

- Ask a question in the Ask a Question box.

- Ask the Office Assistant for help.

- Get help on a particular element you see onscreen with the What's This? tool.

- Use the Contents, Answer Wizard, and Index tabs in the Help window to get help.

- Access the Office on the Web feature to view Web pages containing help information (if you are connected to the Internet).

USING THE ASK A QUESTION BOX

The Ask a Question box is a new way to access the Word Help system. It is also the easiest way to quickly get help. An Ask a Question box resides at the top right of the Word window.

For example, if you are working in Word and wish to view information on how to create a style, type `How do I create a style?` into the Ask a Question box. Then press the **Enter** key. A shortcut menu appears below the Ask a Question box, as shown in Figure 5.1.

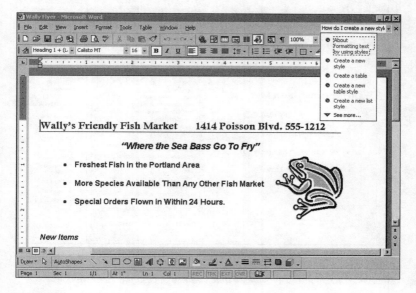

FIGURE 5.1
The Ask a Question box provides a list of Help topics that you can quickly access.

To access one of the Help topics supplied on the shortcut menu, click that particular topic. The Help window opens with topical matches for the keyword or phrase displayed.

In the case of the "styles" question used in Figure 5.1 you could select **Create a new style** from the shortcut menu that appears. This opens the help window and displays help on how to create a Word style (see Figure 5.2).

In the Help window, you can use the links provided to navigate the Help system. You can also use the Contents, Answer Wizard, and Index tabs to find additional information or look for new information in the Help window. You will learn more about these different Help window tabs later in this lesson.

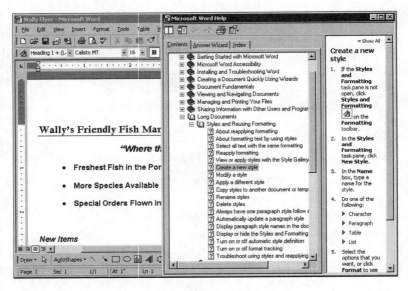

FIGURE 5.2
The Ask a Question box provides a quick way to access the Help window.

USING THE OFFICE ASSISTANT

Another way to get help in Word is to use the Office Assistant. The Office Assistant supplies the same type of access to the Help system as the Ask a Question box. You ask the Office Assistant a question, and it supplies you with a list of possible answers that provide links to various Help topics. The next two sections discuss how to use the Office Assistant.

TURNING THE OFFICE ASSISTANT ON AND OFF

By default, the Office Assistant is off. To show the Office Assistant in your application window, select the **Help** menu and then select **Show the Office Assistant**.

You can also quickly hide the Office Assistant if you no longer want it in your application window. Right-click the Office Assistant and select **Hide**. If you want to get rid of the Office Assistant completely so it isn't activated when you select the Help feature, right-click the Office Assistant and select **Options**. Clear the **Use the Office Assistant** check box, and then click **OK**. You can always get the Office Assistant back by selecting **Help** and then **Show Office Assistant**.

ASKING THE OFFICE ASSISTANT A QUESTION

When you click the Office Assistant, a balloon appears above it. Type a question into the text box. For example, you might type **How do I print?** for help printing your work. Click the **Search** button.

The Office Assistant provides some topics that reference Help topics in the Help system. Click the option that best describes what you're trying to do. The Help window appears, containing more detailed information. Use the Help window to get the exact information that you need.

Although not everyone likes the Office Assistant because having it enabled means that it is always sitting in your Word window, it can be useful at times. For example, when you access particular features in Word, the Office Assistant can automatically provide you with context-sensitive help on that particular feature. If you are brand new to Microsoft Word, you might want to use the Office Assistant to help you learn the various provides.

TIP

> **Select Your Own Office Assistant**   Several different Office Assistants are available in Microsoft Office. To select your favorite, click the Office Assistant and select the **Options** button. On the Office Assistant dialog box that appears, select the **Gallery** tab. Click the **Next** button repeatedly to see the different Office Assistants that are available. When you locate the assistant you want to use, click **OK**.

USING THE HELP WINDOW

You can also forgo either the Type a Question box or the Office
Assistant and get your help directly from the Help window. To directly
access the Help window, select **Help** and then the help command for
the application you are using, such as **Microsoft Word Help.** You can
also press the **F1** key to make the Help window appear.

The Help window provides two panes. The pane on the left provides
three tabs: Contents, Answer Wizard, and Index. The right pane of the
Help window provides either help subject matter or links to different
Help topics. It functions a great deal like a Web browser window.
Click a link to a particular body of information and that information
appears in the right pane.

The first thing that you should do is maximize the Help window by
clicking its **Maximize** button. This makes it easier to locate and read
the information that the Help system provides (see Figure 5.3).

When you first open the Help window, a group of links in the right
pane provides you with access to information about new Word features and other links, such as a link to Microsoft's Office Web site.
Next, take a look at how you can take advantage of different ways to
find information in the Help window: the Contents tab, the Answer
Wizard tab, and the Index tab.

TIP

> **View the Help Window Tabs**   If you don't see the dif-
> ferent tabs in the Help window, click the **Show** button
> on the Help window toolbar.

USING THE CONTENTS TAB

The Contents tab of the Help system is a series of books you can
open. Each book has one or more Help topics in it, which appear as

pages or chapters. To select a Help topic from the Contents tab, follow these steps:

1. In the Help window, click the **Contents** tab on the left side of the Help window.

2. Find the book that describes, in broad terms, the subject for which you need help.

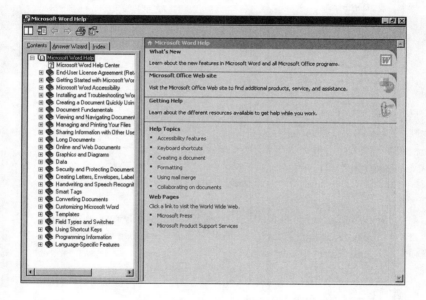

FIGURE 5.3
The Help window provides access to all the help information provided for Word.

3. Double-click the book, and a list of Help topics appears below the book, as shown in Figure 5.4.

4. Click one of the pages (the pages contain a question mark) under a Help topic to display it in the right pane of the Help window.

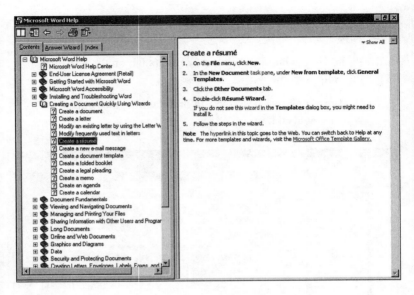

FIGURE 5.4
Use the Contents tab to browse through the various Help topics.

5. When you finish reading a topic, select another topic on the Contents tab or click the Help window's **Close (x)** button to exit Help.

USING THE ANSWER WIZARD

Another way to get help in the Help window is to use the Answer Wizard. The Answer Wizard works the same as the Ask a Question box or the Office Assistant; you ask the wizard questions and it supplies you with a list of topics that relate to your question. Click one of the choices provided to view help in the Help window.

To get help using the Answer Wizard, follow these steps:

1. Click the **Answer Wizard** tab in the Help window.

2. Type your question into the What Would You Like to Do? box. For example, you might type the question, **How do I format text?**

3. After typing your question, click the **Search** button. A list of topics appears in the Select Topic to Display box. Select a particular topic, and its information appears in the right pane of the Help window, as shown in Figure 5.5.

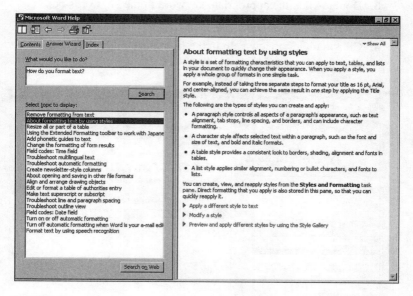

FIGURE 5.5
Search for help in the Help window using the Answer Wizard tab.

TIP

> **Print Help**   If you want to print information provided in the Help window, click the **Print** icon on the Help toolbar.

USING THE INDEX

The Index is an alphabetical listing of every Help topic available. It's like an index in a book.

Follow these steps to use the index:

1. In the Help window, click the **Index** tab.

2. Type the first few letters of the topic for which you are looking. The Or Choose Keywords box jumps quickly to a keyword that contains the characters you have typed.

3. Double-click the appropriate keyword in the keywords box. Topics for that keyword appear in the Choose a Topic box.

4. Click a topic to view help in the right pane of the Help window (see Figure 5.6).

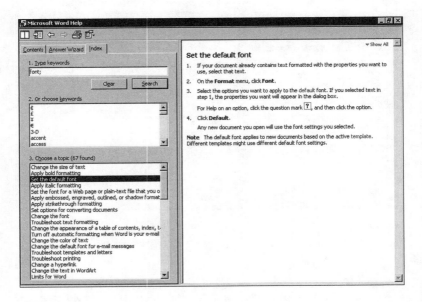

FIGURE 5.6
Use the Index tab to get help in the Help window.

> **Navigation Help Topics**   You can move from topic to topic in the right pane of the Help window by clicking the various links that are provided there. Some topics are collapsed. Click the triangle next to the topic to expand the topic and view the help provided.

GETTING HELP WITH SCREEN ELEMENTS

If you wonder about the function of a particular button or tool on the Word screen, wonder no more. Just follow these steps to learn about this part of Help:

1. Select **Help** and then **What's This?** or press **Shift+F1**. The mouse pointer changes to an arrow with a question mark.

2. Click the screen element for which you want help. A box appears explaining the element.

> **Take Advantage of ScreenTips**   Another Help feature provided by the Office applications is the ScreenTip. All the buttons on the different toolbars provided by Word have a ScreenTip. Place the mouse on a particular button or icon, and the name of the item (which often helps you determine its function) appears in a ScreenTip.

In this lesson you learned how to access the Word Help feature. In the next lesson you will work with proofreading tools such as the Word spell checker, grammar checker, and the AutoCorrect feature.

LESSON 6
Using Proofreading Tools

In this lesson, you learn to check your documents for errors such as misspellings and improper grammar. You work with the spell checker and grammar checker and learn how to find synonyms with the thesaurus, how to proof your document as you type, and how to use the AutoCorrect feature.

PROOFING AS YOU TYPE

Word offers several excellent features for helping you to create error-free documents. Each of these features—the spell checker, the grammar checker, and the thesaurus—are explored in this lesson. Word also gives you the option of checking your spelling and grammar automatically as you type. You can also use the AutoCorrect feature to automatically make some proofing changes for you (for more about AutoCorrect, see "Working with AutoCorrect" in this lesson).

Proofing as you type simply means that errors in spelling and grammar can be automatically flagged as you enter text into your document. This enables you to quickly and immediately correct errors as you build your document.

When you proof as you type, spelling errors—words not found in the Word dictionary file or in your custom dictionary file—are flagged with a wavy red underline. Errors in grammar are underlined with a wavy green line. Spelling and grammar errors marked in this way can be corrected immediately, or you can correct them collectively by running the spelling and grammar checking features after you have finished entering all the text. For information on using the Spelling and

Grammar Checker on a completed document, see the section "Using the Spelling and Grammar Checker," found later in this lesson.

The check-as-you-type features are turned on in Word by default. To change the defaults associated with the automatic spelling and grammar checking features (or to turn them off completely), follow these steps:

1. Select the **Tools** menu and then choose **Options**. The Options dialog box opens.

2. Make sure the **Spelling and Grammar** tab is selected, as shown in Figure 6.1.

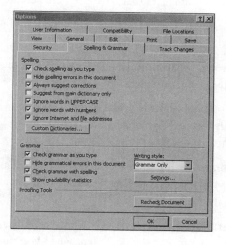

FIGURE 6.1
You can turn the automatic spelling and grammar checking options on or off in the Options dialog box.

3. To toggle the automatic spelling checker on or off, click the **Check Spelling As You Type** check box in the Spelling area of the dialog box.

4. To toggle the automatic grammar checker on or off, click the **Check Grammar As You Type** check box in the Grammar area of the dialog box (near the bottom).

Several other options are also available in this dialog box that relate to how the Spelling and Grammar features operate when you use them in Word.

- **Hide spelling errors in this document**—This option hides the wavy red lines that flag misspellings in the document.

- **Always suggest corrections**—This option provides a list of suggested corrections for each misspelled word when the spell checker is used.

- **Suggest from main dictionary only**—This option uses only the main dictionary for spell checking the document. Any customized dictionaries that have been created are ignored.

- **Ignore words in UPPERCASE**—This option ignores uppercase words in the document.

- **Ignore words with numbers**—This option ignores combinations of text and numbers in the document.

- **Ignore Internet and file addresses**—This option ignores Web addresses and filenames (such as C:\my documents\joe.doc).

- **Hide grammatical errors in the document**—This option hides the wavy green line that marks potential grammatical errors in the document.

- **Check grammar with spelling**—This option is used to check the grammar in the document when you run the spell checker.

- **Show readability statistics**—This option is used to display different readability statistics that show you the readability level and grade level of your text.

After you have finished making your selections in the Options dialog box, click **OK**.

With the check-as-you-type options enabled, suspected misspellings and grammatical errors are flagged with the appropriate colored wavy line.

CORRECTING INDIVIDUAL SPELLING ERRORS

As mentioned, Word marks all words not found in its dictionary with a wavy red line. Because Word's dictionary isn't entirely complete, you might find that it marks correct words as misspelled. To correct words flagged as misspelled (whether they are or not), follow these steps:

1. Place the mouse pointer on the flagged word and click the right mouse button. A shortcut menu appears, as shown in Figure 6.2.

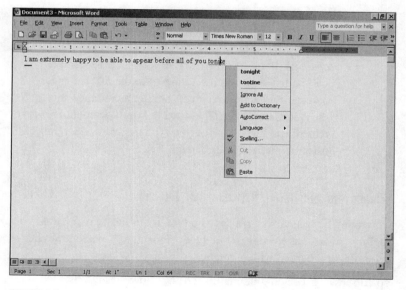

FIGURE 6.2
Right-click any flagged word to get a list of suggested spellings.

2. Word provides a list of possible correct spellings when it encounters a word not in its dictionary. If the correct spelling

for the word you want appears in the list, simply click it, and Word replaces the incorrect spelling with the correct one.

If the flagged word is correctly spelled (and just not in Word's dictionary) or the correct spelling is not in the suggestions list, you have three other options:

- If the word is correct and you don't want it flagged at all in the current document, you can click **Ignore All** and the wavy red line will be removed from all occurrences of the word.

- If the word is correct and you don't want it flagged in this or any other document, you can add the word to the dictionary file; click **Add**.

- If you find that you constantly misspell the word as it currently appears in your document, you can add the word to the AutoCorrect list (discussed later in this chapter). Point to **AutoCorrect**. Suggested spellings will be listed. Select a spelling from the list; the incorrect spelling and the correct spelling are entered into the AutoCorrect list. The word in your document is corrected, and the next time you type the word incorrectly, it is automatically corrected.

CORRECTING INDIVIDUAL GRAMMATICAL ERRORS

Correcting grammatical errors as you type is similar to correcting spelling errors that are flagged in the document. Suspected grammatical errors are marked with a green wavy line.

To correct a suspected grammatical error, follow these steps:

1. Right-click text blocks marked with the green wavy line.

2. The shortcut menu that appears might offer you a list of grammatically correct phrases. Select the phrase that corrects your text entry.

3. If your text is not incorrect grammatically or requires that
you manually make any necessary changes, click **Ignore**.

As soon as you make a selection from the shortcut menu or click
Ignore, the shortcut menu closes. You can then continue working on
your document.

USING THE SPELLING AND GRAMMAR CHECKER

You might prefer not to correct spelling and grammatical errors as you
type. If you're a touch typist, you might not even notice Word has
flagged a word or sentence as incorrect. Waiting to correct the document until you have finished composing enables you to concentrate on
getting your thoughts down without interruption. Then, you can check
the entire document upon completion.

To use the Word Spelling and Grammar feature, follow these steps:

1. Select **Tools, Spelling and Grammar,** or click the **Spelling
and Grammar** button on the toolbar. The Spelling and
Grammar dialog box appears as shown in Figure 6.3.

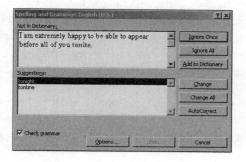

FIGURE 6.3
The Spelling and Grammar dialog box displays the suspected spelling and gram-
mar errors in your document and offers you options for correcting them.

2. Words not found in the dictionary are flagged, and the text in which the word is contained is displayed in the Not in Dictionary box. You can manually correct the highlighted word in the box and then click **Change** to correct the word in the document. The following are other options available for the flagged word:

- Select the appropriate selection for the flagged word from the Suggestion box and click **Change**. If you want to correct all occurrences of the misspelled word (assuming you have consistently and knowingly mis-spelled it), click **Change All**.

- Ignore the flagged word if it is correctly spelled. Click **Ignore Once** to ignore this occurrence of the word, or click **Ignore All** to ignore all occurrences of the word in the document.

- You can also add the word to the dictionary; just click **Add**.

- If you would rather add the misspelled word and an appropriate correct spelling to the AutoCorrect feature, click **AutoCorrect**; the word is corrected, and future insertions of the word (even in other documents when they're opened) with the incorrect spelling are automatically corrected.

Whichever selection you make, the word is dealt with appropriately and the spelling checker moves on to the next flagged word. Make your selection either to correct or to ignore the word, as previously outlined.

If the Check Grammar check box in the Spelling and Grammar dialog box is selected, Word also checks the grammar in your document.

When the Spelling and Grammar dialog box flags a grammatical error in the document, the suspected error appears in the text box at the top of the Spelling and Grammar dialog box with a heading that describes the type of error. Figure 6.4 shows a sentence fragment that has been caught by the grammar checker.

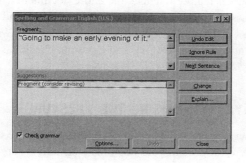

FIGURE 6.4
The grammar checker flags suspected grammatical errors and offers suggestions and possible fixes for the problem.

Suggested corrections, if available, appear in the Suggestions box. In the case of the fragment, the suggestion is to consider revising the fragment. In other cases, more suggestions with actual sentence revisions might appear in this box. If present, select the appropriate revision and click **Change**.

You are also presented with different ignore options for flagged grammatical errors:

- You can choose to ignore the suspected grammatical error by clicking **Ignore**. This ignores only the currently flagged error.

- In some cases, **Ignore All** is also an option. If you click **Ignore All**, the grammar checker ignores all occurrences of this same grammatical error in the rest of the document.

- Word also provides you with the option of ignoring the actual grammar rule that was used to flag the current grammatical error; click **Ignore Rule** to do this throughout the document. This means that any error (not just the current error) that is flagged because of that particular rule (fragment or long sentence, for example is not flagged as a grammatical error.

Use the Grammar feature to check the entire document using the options discussed in this section. When you reach the end of the document and the Grammar check is complete, a dialog box will appear letting you know that the spelling and grammar check has been completed.

FINDING SYNONYMS USING THE THESAURUS

The Word thesaurus provides you with a tool that can be used to find synonyms for the words in your document. Synonyms are words that mean the same thing. Because the thesaurus can generate a list of synonyms for nearly any word in your document, you can avoid the constant use of a particular descriptive adjective (such as "excellent") and add some depth to the vocabulary that appears in your document.

 TIP

The Thesaurus Also Lists Antonyms   Depending on the word you select to find synonyms, you might find that a list of antonyms—words that mean the opposite—are also provided. Antonyms are marked with (antonym) to the right of the suggested word.

To use the thesaurus, follow these steps:

1. Place the insertion point on the word for which you want to find a synonym.

2. Select the **Tools** menu, point at **Language,** and then select **Thesaurus**. The Thesaurus dialog box appears as shown in Figure 6.5.

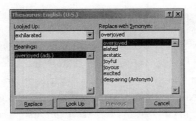

FIGURE 6.5
The Thesaurus dialog box offers a list of synonyms for the selected word.

3. To replace the word with a synonym, select the synonym in the synonym list, and then click **Replace**.

4. You can also choose to see a list of synonyms for any of the words listed in the synonym list. Select the word, and then click **Look Up**. This can provide a greater number of possible words to use when you replace the particular word in your document. The word in your document might be less close in meaning to the synonyms provided on the synonym list.

After you have selected a synonym and clicked **Replace**, the word is replaced in the document and the Thesaurus dialog box closes.

TIP

Right-Click for Synonyms   A quick way to check for a list of synonyms for a word is to right-click that word in your document and then select **Synonyms** from the shortcut menu. A list of synonyms (if available for that word) appears. Select the appropriate word on the list to replace the currently selected word. Words flagged as misspelled or in a sentence marked as a grammatical error will not provide a list of synonyms when you right-click them.

WORKING WITH AUTOCORRECT

Some of your misspelled words are automatically corrected as you type. This is done by the AutoCorrect feature that uses a list of common spelling errors and typos to correct entries in your documents. For example, Word has already arranged to have the incorrect spelling of "t-e-h" to be replaced with "the." You can also add your own words to the AutoCorrect feature. For example, if you always spell aardvark as ardvark, you can set up AutoCorrect to correct this spelling error every time you type it.

You've already seen that the Spelling feature provides you with the option of placing misspelled words into the AutoCorrect library. You can also manually enter pairs of words (the incorrect and correct spellings) into the AutoCorrect dialog box.

To place words in the AutoCorrect list, follow these steps:

1. Click the **Tools** menu, and then click **AutoCorrect Options**. The AutoCorrect dialog box appears as shown in Figure 6.6.

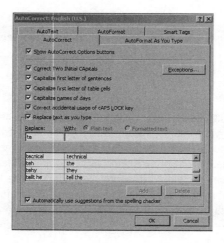

FIGURE 6.6
The AutoCorrect feature enables you to build a list of commonly misspelled words for automatic correction.

2. In the **Replace** box, enter the word as you misspell it. In the **With** box enter the correct spelling of the word.

3. Click **Add** to add the entry to the AutoCorrect list.

4. When you have completed adding entries, click **OK** to close the dialog box.

Now when you misspell the word, Word corrects it for you automatically. You can also use the AutoCorrect dialog box to delete AutoCorrect entries that you do not use (highlight the entry and click **Delete**) or that inadvertently correct items that you want to have in your document (clear the applicable check box).

This feature can also be used to help speed your typing along. For example, suppose that you are writing a technical paper that includes a long organizational name, such as the National Museum of American Art. If you tell the AutoCorrect feature to replace "nmaa" with "National Museum of American Art," it saves you a lot of typing.

TIP

Override the AutoCorrect Feature   If you type a text entry that is automatically changed by the AutoCorrect feature but you want it spelled your original way, immediately place your mouse on the corrected text. The AutoCorrect smart tag (it has a lightning bolt symbol on it) appears. When you click this smart tag's arrow, you can choose to return the word to its original text, among other options.

In this lesson, you learned how to proof your documents as you type. You also learned to use the Spelling and Grammar feature and select synonyms for words in your document using the thesaurus. You also explored the use of the AutoCorrect feature. In the next lesson, you will learn how to change the look of your documents using fonts and how to align text in your documents.

LESSON 7
Changing How Text Looks

In this lesson, you learn basic ways to change the look of your text. You work with fonts and learn how to change font attributes. You also work with text alignment, such as centering and right justification.

UNDERSTANDING FONTS

When you work in Word, you want to be able to control the look of the text in the documents that you create. The size and appearance of the text is controlled for the most part by the font or fonts you choose to use in the document. Each available font has a particular style or typeface. A variety of fonts exists, with names such as Arial, Courier, Times New Roman, CG Times, Bookman Old Style, and so on; the fonts you can choose depend on the fonts that have been installed on your computer (Windows offers a large number of default fonts; other font families are added when you install Office, and you can purchase software for special lettering and printing projects). Each font has a particular look and feel that makes it unique.

TIP

Keep Your Business Documents Standard   The standard point size for most business documents is 12 point, which is 1/6 of an inch tall. So, when selecting a new font, it's generally a good idea to make sure that you use 12 point for documents such as business letters and memos.

You can change the font or fonts used in a document whenever you have the need, and you can also manipulate the size of the characters and their attributes, including bold, underlining, and italic. You can select a new font before you begin typing your document, or you can select text and change its fonts and text attributes at any time.

CHANGING FONT ATTRIBUTES

The easiest way to change font attributes is through the use of the buttons provided on the Word Formatting toolbar. Figure 7.1 shows the Word Formatting toolbar with some of the most common font attribute buttons displayed.

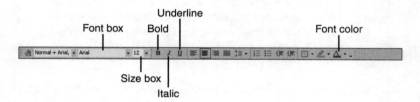

FIGURE 7.1
The Word Formatting toolbar gives you quick access to control the font attributes in your documents.

You can quickly change the font of selected text by clicking the **Font** box and selecting a new font from the list that appears. Other attributes, such as bold, italic, and underline, require that you select the text and then click the appropriate button once to add that attribute to the text. For example, you might want to apply special formatting to a heading so that it stands out from the rest of the text. You can do that by adding bold to the text.

To add bold to text in a document, follow these steps:

1. **Select** the word or other text to be bold.

2. Click the **Bold** button on the Formatting toolbar. The text appears in bold.

B

3. Click any other part of the document to deselect the text and view the results of your formatting.

You can use this same technique to underline and italicize text in your documents.

TIP

>**I Don't Have Those Buttons on My Toolbar**   Click the **Toolbar Options** drop-down arrow, point at **Add or Remove Buttons**, and then select the name of the toolbar to which you want to add the buttons (such as the Formatting toolbar). From the drop-down list, select the buttons that you want to add to the Formatting toolbar. If you don't see the Formatting toolbar at all, right-click any of the toolbars and select **Formatting** on the menu that appears.

You can also use the various font buttons to select font attributes for the new text you type into a new document or insert into an existing document. Select the appropriate font attributes on the Formatting toolbar, and then type the text. To turn off a particular attribute, such as bold or italic, click the appropriate button a second time. To change to a new font or size, use the appropriate drop-down box.

When you are typing in a document, you might find that selecting font attributes from the toolbar actually slows you down because you must remove one hand from the keyboard to use the mouse to make your selection. You can also turn on or off a number of the formatting attributes using shortcut keys on the keyboard. Table 7.1 shows some of the common keyboard shortcuts for formatting attributes.

TABLE 7.1   Font Attribute Shortcut Keys

Attribute	Shortcut Keys
Bold	Ctrl+B
Italic	Ctrl+I

TABLE 7.1   (continued)

Attribute	Shortcut Keys
Underline	Ctrl+U
Double underline	Ctrl+Shift+D
Subscript	Ctrl+equal sign (=)
Superscript	Ctrl+Shift+plus sign (+)

To use any of the shortcut key combinations, press the keys shown simultaneously to turn the attribute on, and then repeat the key sequence to turn the attribute off. For example, to turn on bold while you are typing, press the **Ctrl** key and the **B** key at the same time. Press these keys again to turn the bold off.

WORKING IN THE FONT DIALOG BOX

Although the Formatting toolbar certainly provides the quickest avenue for controlling various font attributes, such as the font and the font size, you can access several more font attributes in the Font dialog box. The Font dialog box gives you control over common attributes, such as font, font size, bold, and so on, and it also provides you with control over special font attributes, such as superscript, subscript, and strikethrough.

To open the Font dialog box, click the **Format** menu and then select **Font**. The Font dialog box appears, as shown in Figure 7.2.

As you can see, the Font dialog box enables you to choose from several font attributes. You can control the font, the font style, and other character attributes such as strikethrough, superscript, and shadow, as shown next.

- To change the font, click the **Font** drop-down box and select the new font by name.

- To change the font style to italic, bold, or bold italic, make the appropriate selection in the **Font Style** box.

- To change the size of the font, select the appropriate size in the **Size** scroll box.

- For underlining, click the **Underline Style** drop-down box and select an underlining style.

- To change the color of the font, click the **Font Color** drop-down box and select a new color.

- To select any special effects, such as strikethrough, super-script, or shadow, select the appropriate check box in the lower half of the dialog box.

FIGURE 7.2
The Font dialog box provides you with control over several font attributes not found on the Formatting toolbar.

As you make the various selections in the Font dialog box, a sample of what the text will look like appears in the Preview box at the bottom of the dialog box. After you have made all your selections in the Font dialog box, click **OK**.

TIP

> **Change the Default Font** To change the default font that you use for your documents (those created using the current or desired template), select the font attributes in the Font dialog box and then click the **Default** button at the lower left of the dialog box. Click **Yes** when Word asks for a confirmation of the change.

ALIGNING TEXT

Another important basic attribute of the text in your documents is how that text is oriented on the page. When you first start typing in a new document, all the text begins at the left margin and moves to the right as you type; this means the text is left-justified using the default align left feature. Left-justified text is characterized by text that is straight or unvarying on the left margin but has a ragged right-edged margin.

Text that serves a special function in a document, such as a heading, would probably stand out better in the document if it were placed differently than the rest of the text. Word makes it easy for you to change the alignment of any text paragraph. Several alignment possibilities are available:

- **Align Left**—The default margin placement for normal text that is aligned on the left.

- **Align Right**—Text is aligned at the right margin and text lines show a ragged left edge.

- **Center**—The text is centered between the left and right margins of the page (with both margins having irregular edges).

- **Justify**—The text is spaced irregularly across each line so that both the left and the right margins are straight edged and uniform (often used in printed publications such as the daily newspapers).

CAUTION

Remember How Word Sees a Paragraph Any text followed by a paragraph mark—created when you press the **Enter** key—is considered a separate paragraph in Word. This means that when you use alignment features, such as those discussed in this section, only the paragraph that currently holds the insertion point will be affected by the alignment command that you select (such as Center). If you need to align multiple lines that are in separate paragraphs, select that text before selecting the alignment command.

Figure 7.3 shows examples of each of the alignment possibilities.

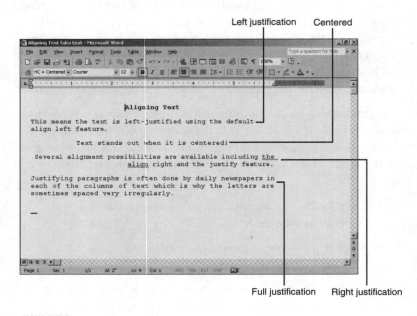

FIGURE 7.3
You can align the text in your document to suit your particular needs on a document page.

The easiest way to change the alignment of text in the document is to use the alignment buttons on the Formatting toolbar. Also, a button exists in the Paragraph dialog box for each of the alignment possibilities. Table 7.2 shows the buttons and their functions.

TABLE 7.2   Alignment Icons on the Formatting Toolbar

Button	Justification
	Align left
	Center
	Align right
	Justify (full justification)

These justification buttons can be used to align new text or selected text. Again, if you are typing new text with a particular justification, your selected justification will still be in force even after you press Enter. You must change the justification as needed.

ALIGNING TEXT WITH CLICK AND TYPE

Word offers a unique and quick way to insert and align text (or to insert graphics, tables, and other items) in a blank area of a document. Before entering text or another item, place the mouse pointer on a blank line on the page. As you move the mouse pointer from right to left on the blank line, the pointer (or I-beam, in this case) changes shapes as you move it, denoting a particular line alignment. This makes it very easy to center or right align the insertion point before you insert the text or other item.

CAUTION

Click and Type Option Must Be On   To use Click and Type, you must also make sure that the **Enable Click and Type** box is selected on the **Edit** tab of the Options dialog box (select **Tools** and then **Options** to open this dialog box).

To use the Click and Type feature, you must be in the Print Layout or Web Layout view. The feature is not available in the Normal view. To switch to the Print Layout or Web Layout view, select **View**, and then select the appropriate view from the View menu.

Then, to use Click and Type to align your new text, follow these steps:

1. Move the mouse pointer toward the area of the page where you want to place the insertion point. The pointer icon changes to

   - Center (the centering pointer appears)

   - Right (the align-right pointer appears)

2. After the mouse pointer shows the centering or right-align icon, double-click in the document. The insertion point moves to the selected justification.

3. Type your new text.

After you've typed the centered or right-aligned text and you've pressed **Enter** to create a new line, you can return to left justification by placing the mouse to the left of the line (the align-left icon appears on the mouse pointer) and double-clicking.

AUTOMATICALLY DETECTING FORMATTING INCONSISTENCIES

Word 2002 offers a new feature that marks formatting inconsistencies in your document. This allows you to make sure that the text in your document is formatted as you intended. The Detect Formatting feature keeps track of the formatting in your document and can also be configured to flag any formatting inconsistencies.

To configure the Detect Formatting feature to flag formatting inconsistencies, follow these steps:

1. Select **Tools** and then select **Options**. The Options dialog box opens.

2. On the Options dialog box, select the **Edit** tab.

3. Under Editing options, select the **Keep track of Formatting** check box, if it is not already selected. Also select the **Mark Formatting Inconsistencies** check box.

4. Click **OK** to close the Options dialog box.

Now, formatting inconsistencies will be marked with a wavy blue line as you type. When you find a word or paragraph that has been flagged with the wavy blue line, right-click the word or paragraph. A shortcut menu appears as shown in Figure 7.4.

Use the menu choices on the shortcut menu to either replace the direct formatting with an available style or ignore the direct formatting occurrence. To ignore this formatting occurrence, click **Ignore Once**. If you want all formatting occurrences that have been flagged by the Detect Formatting feature to be ignored in the document, click the **Ignore Rule** choice on the shortcut menu.

Be advised that the Detect Formatting feature doesn't always catch formatting errors. For example, if you have most of your text in a 12-point font, some font that you might have inadvertently formatted for 14 point won't necessarily be flagged. Word assumes you might be using the 14 point for a heading or other special text.

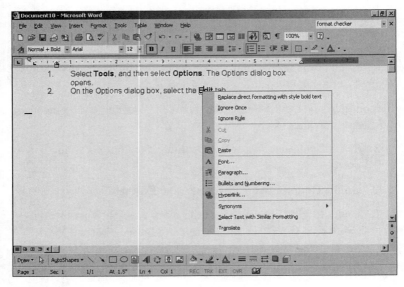

FIGURE 7.4
You can have formatting inconsistencies flagged in your documents.

The Detect Formatting feature is best at detecting direct formatting changes that you have made to text in a document (such as directly adding bold to text, as shown in Figure 7.4), where other text that has been bolded has been formatted using a "bold" style that you created (styles are covered in Lesson 12, "Working with Styles"). The inconsistency that Word picks up on is that you didn't use the style to bold the item as you had done in the rest of the document.

In this lesson, you learned how change the font and font size in your document and work with various font attributes, such as bold, italic, and underline. You also learned how to align text in your document and worked with the various justification options. In the next lesson, you will learn how to use borders and colors to emphasize text in your documents.

LESSON 8
Using Borders and Colors

In this lesson, you learn how to use borders and colors to emphasize text in your documents.

ADDING BORDERS TO TEXT

In Lesson 7, "Changing How Text Looks," you learned that you can use various font attributes, such as font size, bold, italic, and under-line, to emphasize and otherwise denote certain text in your document. You also learned that alignment, such as centering, can be used to set off certain text lines on a page. Word provides you with the capability to add borders to your text and even place a shadow on the edge of a border for greater emphasis.

A border can be placed around any text paragraph (any line followed by a paragraph mark). This means that one line of text or several lines of text can have a border placed around them.

TIP

> ¶ **Remember How Word Views a Paragraph** Whenever you type a line or several lines of text and then press **Enter**, you are placing an end-of-paragraph mark at the end of the text. Word views any line or lines followed by a paragraph mark as a separate paragraph. If you need to view the paragraph marks in your document, click the **Show/Hide** button on the Word Standard toolbar.

To place a border around a text paragraph, follow these steps:

1. Place the insertion point in the paragraph that you want to place the border around. If you want to place a border around multiple paragraphs, select all the paragraphs.

2. Select the **Format** menu, and then **Borders and Shading**. The Borders and Shading dialog box appears, as shown in Figure 8.1.

FIGURE 8.1

Click here to put a line over the text.

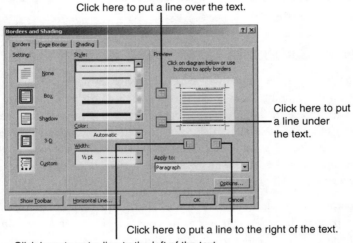

Click here to put a line under the text.

Click here to put a line to the right of the text.

Click here to put a line to the left of the text.

The Borders and Shading dialog box enables you to place a border around your text.

3. Make sure the **Borders** tab is selected on the dialog box. You are provided with several settings for how the border should appear around the text.

4. In the Setting area of the dialog box, select the type of box you want around your text; choose **Box**, **Shadow**, **3-D**, or **Custom** by clicking the appropriate setting sample. The Custom option enables you to create a border that uses different line styles for the various sides of the border.

TIP

> **Removing a Border from a Paragraph**   If you want to remove the border from a paragraph, choose **None** in the Setting area of the Borders and Shading dialog box.

5. Several line styles are available for your border. Click the **Style** scroll box to scroll through the various line styles, and then click the style you want to use.

6. To change the color of the border lines, click the **Color** drop-down arrow and select a color from the color palette that appears.

7. As you select the various parameters for your border (in cases where you have selected Box, Shadow, or 3-D as the border setting), you can view a preview of the border in the Preview box. The Preview box also makes it easy for you to place an incomplete border around a paragraph in cases where you might only want a line above or below the text (refer to Figure 8.1).

8. When you have finished selecting the settings for the border, click the **OK** button. The border appears around the paragraph or paragraphs in the document, as shown in Figure 8.2.

You also can quickly place a border around a paragraph or other selected text by using the Tables and Borders toolbar. Right-click anywhere on one of the currently shown toolbars and select **Tables and Borders** from the toolbar list. The Tables and Borders toolbar appears in the document window. Figure 8.3 shows the Tables and Borders toolbar.

CAUTION

Borders Around More Than One Paragraph If you select several paragraphs that are using the same style and indents, Word places one border around all the paragraphs. If you want separate borders around the paragraphs, assign a border to them one at a time. For more discussion about indents, see Lesson 9, "Working with Tabs and Indents." You can find more information about styles in Lesson 11, "Working with Margins, Pages, and Line Spacing."

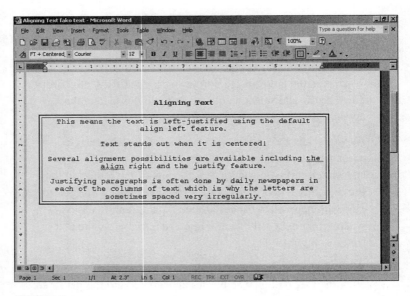

FIGURE 8.2
A border appears around the selected paragraph after you set the border parameters in the Borders and Shading dialog box.

 To apply a border to a paragraph, make sure the insertion point is in the paragraph, and then click the **Borders** drop-down button on the Tables and Borders toolbar. From the border list provided, select the type of border you want to place around the text.

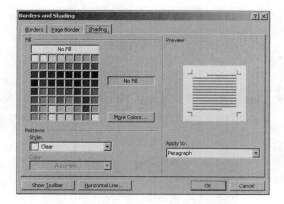

FIGURE 8.3
You can add borders to selected text using the Tables and Borders toolbar.

PLACING A BORDER AROUND A PAGE

If you find that you would like to place a border around an entire page or pages in your document, you need to use the Page Border feature.

Follow these steps to place a border around the entire page:

1. Open the Borders and Shading dialog box (click the **Format** menu and select **Borders and Shading**) and click the **Page Border** tab (see Figure 8.4).

2. Select the **Border** setting and style as you would for a paragraph border.

3. Click the **Apply To** list drop-down arrow and select one of the following:

   • **Whole Document**—Places a border around each page in the document.

- **This Section**—Places a border around each page in the current section of the document.

- **This Section-First Page Only**—Places a border around the first page of the current section.

- **This Section-All Except First Page**—Places a border around each page of the current section except the first page.

FIGURE 8.4
Borders can be placed around an entire page.

To put a border around pages in a section, you must place sections in your document. Sections enable you to break a large document into smaller parts that can have radically different formatting attributes. For more about sections and how to create them, see Lesson 21, "Working with Larger Documents."

PLAIN ENGLISH

Section   A portion of a document that has been defined as a discrete part. Each section can then have different formatting and even headers and footers defined for the section.

ADDING SHADING TO THE PARAGRAPH

You can place a color or a grayscale pattern behind the text in a paragraph or paragraphs. This color or pattern is called shading and can be used with or without a border around the text.

To add shading to text, you must select the text for a particular paragraph—just make sure the insertion point is in the paragraph.

After you've designated the text that you want to place the shading behind, follow these steps:

1. Select **Format, Borders and Shading**. The Borders and Shading dialog box appears.

2. Select the **Shading** tab, as shown in Figure 8.5.

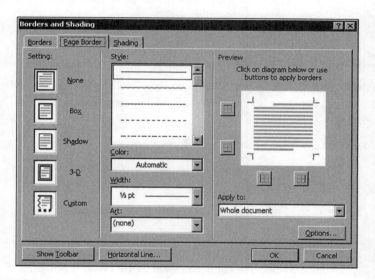

FIGURE 8.5
You can apply shading to a paragraph or selected text.

3. To select a fill color, click one of the colors on the color palette in the **Fill** area.

4. To select a pattern for the fill color, click the **Style** drop-down arrow and select a pattern from the list.

5. Use the **Apply To** drop-down arrow to designate whether the current paragraph or selected text should be shaded.

6. When you have completed your selections, click **OK**.

Your selected text or paragraph will now be shaded.

TIP

Take Advantage of More Colors   If the color you want to use is not shown on the Shading tab, click the **More Colors** button. This opens the Colors dialog box, which provides a huge number of colors on a color palette. You can even click the **Custom** tab on this dialog box and mix your own custom colors.

CHANGING FONT COLORS

When using the shading options, you might find that the current text color does not show up that well on the fill color or pattern that you selected.

To change the color of text, follow these steps:

1. Select the text that you want to change to a different font color.

2. Select the **Format** menu and select **Font**. The Font dialog box appears.

3. In the Font dialog box, click the **Font Color** drop-down arrow and select the color you want to use (Word automatically defaults to black-colored fonts because this is typically what you use in business documents that you print).

4. When you have completed your selection, click **OK**.

You might find that you have to play around with the fill color and the font color to get an ideal combination on the page. Intensity of color typically varies between color printers.

In this lesson, you learned how to place a border around your text and place shading behind text. You also learned how to change the font color for selected text. In the next lesson, you will learn how to set tabs and indents in your documents.

LESSON 9
Working with Tabs and Indents

In this lesson, you learn how to set and use tabs and indents in your documents.

ALIGNING TEXT WITH TABS

Although the left and right alignment of text in your document is governed by the margins set in the document, there are times when you want to align the text to emphasize a list of items or otherwise offset text from the rest of the items on the page. In Lesson 7, "Changing How Text Looks," you worked with centering and justification as a way to change the alignment of text. Another way to align text in a document is to use tabs. Tabs are set every half inch by default in a new document. Every time you press the Tab key on the keyboard, you offset the text line from the left margin one tab stop.

You can use tab stops to align text lines in columns. Word gives you complete control over where the tab stops are set in your document. Word also provides different tabs that enable you to align text in different ways:

- **Left Tab**—Aligns the beginning of the text line at the tab stop

- **Center Tab**—Centers the text line at the tab stop

- **Right Tab**—Right-aligns the text line at the tab stop

- **Decimal Tab**—Lines up numerical entries at their decimal point

Each of these tab types makes it easy for you to create lists that are offset from other text elements in the document. Your tab stops fall between the left and right margins on each page of the document. Each paragraph in the document can potentially have a different set of tab stops with different kinds of tabs set at the stops.

One way to set tabs in your document is using the Tabs dialog box. Select the **Format** menu, and then select **Tabs**. The Tabs dialog box requires that you specify a tab position in the Tab stop position box (the position you specify is the number of inches from the left margin); use the spinner box arrows to specify the position for the tab or type a position directly in the box.

After the tab stop position is set, click the appropriate Alignment option button to select the type of tab you want to create at the tab stop (see Figure 9.1). If you want to have a leader (a repeating element, such as a dash), fill the empty space to the left of the tab stop and select one of the leader option buttons in the Leader box. After you have specified a position and a tab type (and an optional leader), add the tab by clicking **Set**.

As you create the tabs, they will appear in the Tabs list on the left of the dialog box. If you want to remove a particular tab from the list, select it, and then click the **Clear** button. If you want to clear all the tabs listed (and start over), click the **Clear All** button.

After you have finished setting your tabs, click **OK**. Although you can certainly set all the tabs for a document or section in the Tabs dialog box, it is not necessarily the best place to quickly set the tabs for your documents. It does not really provide you with a visual display of how the tabs will look in the document. However, if you are creating tabs that include leading characters (such as dot leaders often seen in a table of contents) and you want to precisely set the tab positions to previously determined settings, the Tabs dialog box gives you complete control over all the settings.

FIGURE 9.1
You can set and remove tab stops in the Tabs dialog box.

SETTING TABS ON THE RULER

An excellent alternative to setting tabs in the Tabs dialog box is to use the Word Ruler and actually set the tabs on the Ruler itself. This enables you to visually check the position of the tab stops and makes it easy for you to change the type of tab at a particular tab stop and delete unwanted tabs.

To view the Ruler in the Word document window, select **View** and then **Ruler**. The Ruler appears at the top of your document.

TIP

> **Quickly View the Ruler**   If the Ruler is not displayed in the Word window, place the mouse pointer at the top of your current document, below the toolbars. If you wait for just a moment, the Ruler drops down onto the document. This allows you to view current tab settings. When you remove the mouse, the Ruler folds up.

To set a tab on the Ruler, click the **Tab** button on the far left of the Ruler to select the tab type (Left, Center, Right, or Decimal). Each time you click the Tab button, you are cycled to the next tab type. If you go past the type of tab you want to set, keep clicking until the tab type appears on the Tab button.

After you have the appropriate tab type selected on the Tab button, place the mouse pointer on the ruler where you want to create the tab stop. Click the mouse and the tab is placed on the ruler. It's that simple.

Figure 9.2 shows the Ruler with each of the tab types set. The figure also shows how text aligns at each of the tab types.

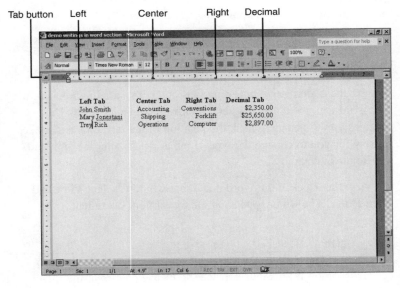

FIGURE 9.2
Setting tabs on the Ruler allows you to view their position and type.

TIP

Moving or Removing Tabs   If you want to delete a tab on the Ruler, use the mouse to drag the tab off the Ruler. If you need to reposition a particular tab, drag it to a new location on the Ruler.

WORKING WITH INDENTS

Although tabs enable you to align text at various tab stops on the Ruler, you might want to indent or offset lines and paragraphs from the left or right margins. Word provides different indent settings that indent the text at particular settings on the Ruler.

PLAIN ENGLISH

Indent   The offset of a particular paragraph or line of text from the left or right margin.

The easiest way to indent a paragraph from the left margin is to use the **Increase Indent** button on the Formatting toolbar. Place the insertion point in the paragraph you want to indent, and then click the **Increase Indent** button on the toolbar. Remember that you can also use the Click and Type feature for left indents (see the previous Lesson 8, "Using Borders and Colors").

Each time you click the button, you are increasing the indent one-half inch. You can also decrease the left indent on a particular paragraph. Click the **Decrease Indent** button on the Formatting toolbar.

SETTING INDENTS ON THE RULER

You can also indent a paragraph from both the left and right margins using the Ruler. The Ruler has a left and right indent marker on the far left and far right, respectively (see Figure 9.3).

To indent a paragraph from the left margin, use the mouse to drag the **Left Indent** marker to the appropriate position. Grab the marker at the very bottom because the top of the marker is the First Line Indent marker. You can also indent a paragraph from the right margin using the Right Indent marker.

Left Indent marker

First Line Indent marker

Right Indent marker

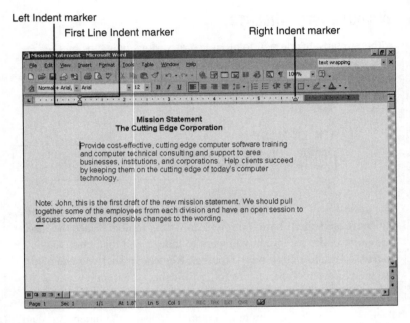

FIGURE 9.3
The Left Indent and Right Indent markers can be used to indent paragraphs from the left and right margins, respectively.

CREATING HANGING INDENTS

The hanging indent is a special kind of indent. The text that wraps under the first line of the paragraph is indented more than the first line. Hanging indents are created by separating the First Line Indent marker from the Left Indent marker on the ruler.

To create a hanging indent, follow these steps:

1. Place the insertion point in the paragraph that you want to indent.

2. Drag the **Left Indent marker** (drag it by the square bottom of the marker) to the position where you want to indent the second and subsequent lines of the paragraph.

3. Drag the **First Line Indent marker** (drag it by the top of the marker) back to the position where you want the first line to begin.

Figure 9.4 shows a paragraph with a hanging indent. You can increase or decrease the offset between the first line and the rest of the paragraph by dragging either the First Line Marker or the Left Indent marker. If you prefer to enter numerical information for your hanging indents, choose the **Indents and Spacing** tab (select **Format** menu and then **Paragraph**) and in the **Special** list under **Indentation**, select **Hanging**. Then, set the amount of space for the hanging indent in the **By** box.

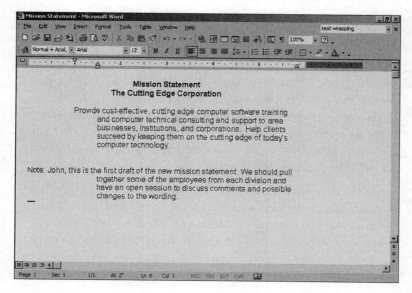

FIGURE 9.4
Hanging indents enable you to offset the indent on the first line of a paragraph and the remainder of the paragraph.

In this lesson, you learned to set tabs in your document using the Tabs dialog box and the Ruler. You also learned how to set indents for your paragraphs. In the next lesson, you will learn how to change the view of your document in the Word window.

LESSON 10
Examining Your Documents in Different Views

In this lesson, you learn how to examine your document using the different document displays offered in Word.

CHANGING THE DOCUMENT DISPLAY

Word provides you with several viewing possibilities as you work on your documents in the Word application window. Each of these display modes provides a different look at your document. For example, the Normal view provides you with a look at all the font and paragraph formatting in the document, but does not give you a view of the document as it would appear on the printed page. Instead, the Print Layout view supplies this viewpoint.

Using the different document views to your advantage can help you visualize and create great-looking documents in Word. Special views are even supplied for creating outlines and creating Web pages in Word. Take advantage of these different views using the View menu. Table 10.1 shows the various views available to you and describes, in general terms, for what they are best used.

TABLE 10.1 The Word Views

View	Typical Use
Normal	Use for general word processing tasks
Web Layout	Use for designing HTML documents and viewing Web pages

TABLE 10.1 (continued)

View	Typical Use
Print Layout	Use for document layout and documents containing graphics and embedded or linked objects
Outline	Use to view document as an outline
Full Screen	Use when you want to use the entire screen to view the document and avoid seeing the toolbars and other marginal information

THE NORMAL VIEW

The Normal view provides you with a view that is perfect for most word processing tasks. It is the default view for Word; however, to change to the Normal view from another view, select **View** and then **Normal**.

TIP

> **■ Switch to Normal with a Click**   You can also change from view to view in Word using the View toolbar in the lower-left corner of the Word window. To go to the Normal view, click the **Normal** icon.

This view displays character and paragraph formatting that you place in the document (see Figure 10.1). Normal view, however, does not display the document headers and footers or show graphics in the document as they will print. Also, items created using the Drawing toolbar are not displayed in the Normal view.

In the Normal view, you see the following:

- Page breaks appear as dashed lines.

- Headers and footers are displayed in a header/footer editing pane (when **Header and Footer** is selected on the **View** menu). Only the header or footer can be edited at this point.

- Footnotes and endnotes are displayed in a footnote or endnote editing pane (when **Footnotes** is selected on the **View** menu). Only the footnote or endnote can be edited at this point.

- Margins and column borders are not displayed in this view.

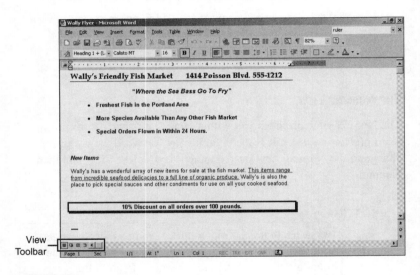

View
Toolbar

FIGURE 10.1
The Normal view shows all the formatting in the document but does not show graphics, margins, and other special elements as they will appear on the printed page.

WEB LAYOUT VIEW

The Web Layout view is perfect for designing *HTML* documents that you want to use as Web pages. The Web Layout view displays your document as it would appear in your Web browser window. To switch to the Web Layout view, select **View**, and then **Web Layout**.

In the Web Layout view, text is wrapped to fit in the window and graphics are placed as they will appear online. Any backgrounds

present on the page are also seen in this view. Figure 10.2 shows a
Web page in the Web Layout view.

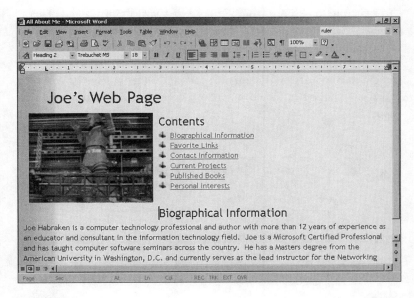

FIGURE 10.2
*The Web Layout view allows you to look at and edit your HTML documents as
they will appear in a Web browser.*

TIP

> 🖻 **Switch to Web Layout View Quickly**   To switch to the
> Web Layout view, click the **Web Layout** icon on the **View**
> toolbar.

The Web Layout view is the perfect view for designing your personal
Web pages or for viewing Web pages using the Web Page Wizard.

PRINT LAYOUT VIEW

The Print Layout view shows your document exactly as it will appear
on the printed page. Working in this view allows you to fine-tune your

document and work with graphic placement and text formatting as you prepare your document for printing.

To switch to the Print Layout view, select **View**, **Print Layout**. This enables you to view headers, footers, footnotes, endnotes, and the margins in your document. Graphics are also positioned and sized as they will appear on the printed page. Figure 10.3 shows the same document that appeared in Figure 10.1 but notice that in Page Layout view, the margins of the document and a graphic in the document appears.

TIP

> **Switch to Print Layout View Quickly**   To switch to the Print Layout view, click the **Print Layout** icon on the **View** toolbar.

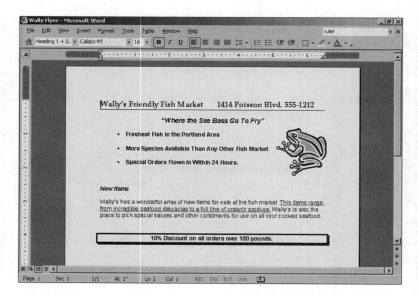

FIGURE 10.3
The Print Layout view enables you to fine-tune your document for printing.

OUTLINE VIEW

The Outline view allows you to create and edit your document in an outline format. Using the Word built-in heading styles is the key to creating the document in this view (for more about styles, see Lesson 11, "Working with Margins, Pages, and Line Spacing"). Each heading (Headings 1, 2, 3, and so on) is treated as a different level in the outline. For example, a heading assigned the Heading 1 style would be a Level 1 heading in the outline. You can promote and demote headings using the appropriate buttons on the Outline toolbar (a special toolbar that appears when you are in Outline view).

The Outline toolbar also provides an Outline Levels drop-down box that allows you to quickly change the level of the text where the insertion point currently resides. These levels coincide with different styles used by the outline feature. For example, Level 1 is equivalent to the Heading 1 style.

You can also collapse and expand the outline to better organize your document. Collapsing the document to all Level 1 Headings allows you to ignore the body text in the document and concentrate on the overall organization of the document.

 TIP

Move a Heading and Associated Text   When you drag a heading to a new position, the subheading and body text associated with the heading move to the new position as well. This makes it very easy for you to reorganize the text in your document.

To change to the Outline view, select **View** and then click **Outline**. You can easily select a heading and the text that is subordinate to it by clicking the hollow plus symbol (+) to the left of the text (see Figure 10.4). After the text is selected, it can be dragged to a new position.

When you have finished creating and editing a document in the Outline view, you can switch to any of the other views (such as the Print Layout view) to see your document in a more typical format.

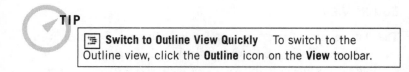

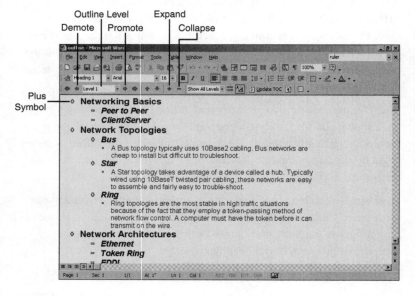

FIGURE 10.4
The Outline view makes it very easy to organize your document by collapsing and expanding different levels.

USING THE FULL SCREEN VIEW

In situations where you want to concentrate on the text and other items in your document, it is great to be able to clear all the visual clutter from the screen (toolbars, scrollbars, and other Word tools) and view only your document. For example, you might be proofreading a particular page and want to place as much of the page's text on the screen as you can. You can switch to a view where your document occupies all the space available on the screen. Select **View** and then **Full Screen**.

You can still add or edit the text in your document when you are in the Full Screen view. You can also quickly return to the previous view you were using (such as Normal view or Print Layout view) before you switched to the Full Screen view. Click the **Close Full Screen** box that appears in the document window to return to the previous view.

Zooming In and Out on Your Document

You can use the Zoom command to zoom in and out on your documents. This allows you to increase the magnification of items on the page, such as small fonts, and allows you to step back (zoom out) from the document to view its general layout.

You can use Zoom in any of the Word views. In Normal, Web Layout, and Outline views, the effect of zooming in or out just changes the magnification of the onscreen elements. When you use Zoom on the Print Layout view, you get a good look at how the document is laid out on the printed page.

To zoom in or out on your current document, select **View**, **Zoom**. The Zoom dialog box appears (see Figure 10.5).

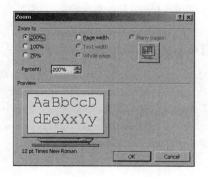

FIGURE 10.5
The Zoom dialog box can be used to change the current zoom level of your document.

A series of option buttons is used to change the zoom setting for the current document. When you click a particular option button (such as the 200% option button), you see a preview of this magnification in the Preview box.

You can also set a custom zoom level in the Percent box. Use the click arrows in the box to increase or decrease the current Zoom percentage. When you have selected the zoom level for the current document, click **OK**.

TIP

> **View Multiple Pages on Your Screen**   When you are in the Print Layout view, you can use the Zoom dialog box to view two or more pages at the same time. Click the **Many Pages** option button (when in Zoom option), and then click the **Computer** icon below the option button. Drag over the page boxes to select the number of pages you want to display, and then click **OK**.

You can also quickly change the zoom level in your current document using the Zoom drop-down box on the Word Standard toolbar. Click the drop-down arrow on the **Zoom** box and select the appropriate zoom level. If you want to set a custom zoom level, select the current zoom percentage on the Zoom box and then type your own value.

WORKING WITH THE DOCUMENT MAP

The Document Map view is somewhat similar to the Outline view in that it gives you a quick reference to the overall structure of your document. A special pane appears in the document window (on the left) that shows the headings in your document. The Document Map can be used to quickly move from one area of a document to another by clicking the appropriate heading.

To open the Document Map, select **View, Document Map**; the map pane appears in the document window (see Figure 10.6). You can change the width of the Document Map pane by placing the mouse on the border between the pane and your document. The mouse arrow changes to a sizing tool—a double-headed arrow. Drag the sizing tool to create a custom Document Map width.

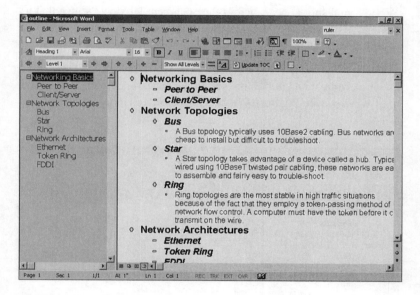

FIGURE 10.6
The Document Map view makes it easy to jump to a particular part of a document by clicking the appropriate heading.

The Document Map pane is available in any of the Word views. When you want to close the Document Map, select **View**, and then **Document Map** to deselect it.

SPLITTING THE DOCUMENT WINDOW

Another useful way to view your documents is to split the current document window into two panes. This allows you to view the same document in both panes, which is particularly useful when you want to view two different parts of the same document.

You can use the two panes to drag and drop information from one part of a document into another. Remember that changes you make in either of the split panes will affect the document.

To split the document screen into two panes, select **Window, Split**. A horizontal split appears across the document window. Notice that as you move the mouse in the document window, the split bar moves with it. Place the mouse where you want to split the document window, and then click the left mouse button.

A set of vertical and horizontal scrollbars appears for each pane in the split window (see Figure 10.7). Use the scrollbars in each pane as needed.

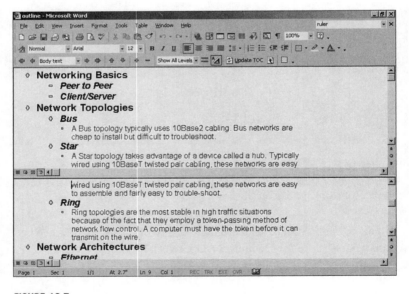

FIGURE 10.7
You can split the document screen to view different areas of a long document.

When you have finished working in the split document window, select **Window** and then **Remove Split**. The splitter bar is removed from the document.

TIP

> **Split a Window Using the Splitter Bar** You can split a document window by manually dragging the splitter bar down into the document window. Place the mouse just above the Up arrow on the vertical scrollbar on the splitter bar. Your mouse becomes a splitter sizing tool. Drag to split the window as needed, and then click the mouse to set the bar.

In this lesson, you learned to take advantage of the various views offered to you by Word. You also learned to zoom in and out on your document and split the document window. In the next lesson, you will learn how to work with margins, line spacing, and line breaks.

Lesson 11

Working with Margins, Pages, and Line Spacing

In this lesson, you learn how to set margins, insert page breaks into your documents, and control line spacing and line breaks in your documents.

Setting Margins

Margins control the amount of whitespace between your text and the edge of a printed page. Four margins—Left, Right, Top, and Bottom—can be set for your pages. The default margin settings for documents based on the Word Normal template are shown in Table 11.1.

TABLE 11.1   Default Margin Settings for the Normal Template

Margin	Setting (in Inches)
Left	1.25
Right	1.25
Top	1
Bottom	1

You can change any of the margin settings for your document or a portion of your document at any time. The Page Setup dialog box provides you with access to all these margin settings. You also have

control over how your margins affect the layout of multiple pages in a
document. For example, you can set up your pages to be laid out in
book folio fashion (two pages arranged horizontally on each piece of
paper) or two pages per sheet arranged vertically.

To change the margin settings for your document, follow these steps:

1. Select **File**, **Page Setup**. The Page Setup dialog box appears
   as shown in Figure 11.1.

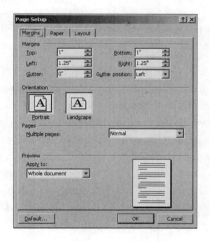

FIGURE 11.1
*Use the Margins tab of the Page Setup dialog box to set your document margins
and arrange them on multiple pages if necessary.*

TIP

> **Margins Can Be Different for Different Parts of the Document**
> You can set different margin settings for different por-
> tions of your document. The easiest way to do this is to
> divide your document into sections. Each section can
> then have a different set of margins. For information on
> creating sections in your documents, see Lesson 21,
> "Working with Larger Documents."

2. Click the **Margins** tab if necessary. You can also double-click in any of the boxes and type in a new value.

CAUTION

> **Maximum and Minimum Margins**   Be advised that your printer defines the minimum margins for a page. Most inkjet printers limit you to a minimum top and bottom margins of .25" and .5", and left and right margins of .25". If you set margins less than the minimum, a dialog box appears letting you know that your margins are outside the printable area of the page. Click the **Fix** button to set the margins to the minimum for your printer.

3. After you have selected the new margin settings, you can apply the margins to the entire document, to a section of the document, or to the document from the current page forward in the document. Using the last choice allows you to have different margin settings in the same document without requiring you to divide the document into sections (for more about sections, see Lesson 21). Click the **Apply To** drop-down box and select **Whole Document** (the default setting), **This Point Forward**, or **This Section** (if available).

4. After you have finished selecting your new margin settings and the amount of the document that they will affect, click **OK**.

TIP

> **Set a Gutter for Bound Documents**   If your document will be bound (left or top) or placed into a three-ring notebook, set a value in the Gutter box to provide extra space for the binding or punch holes. Setting the Mirror Margins (under multiple pages) ensures that margins on facing pages are similar.

The new margins take effect in your document. The best way to view how they will look when you print is to switch to the Print Layout view (if you are not already in this view). Select **View, Print Layout**. The margins you've selected appear on the top, left, right, and bottom of your document in the Word document window.

When you are in the Print Layout view, you can adjust the margins in your document using the Ruler. To view the Ruler, select **View, Ruler**. The vertical ruler is visible in the Print Layout View only.

In the Print Layout view, horizontal and vertical rulers appear in the document window. The margins appear as shaded areas on the edge of the respective ruler. For example, the left margin is a gray-shaded area on the left side of the horizontal ruler (see Figure 11.2).

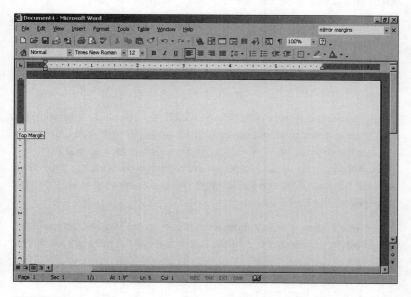

FIGURE 11.2
Drag the respective margin-sizing arrow to increase or decrease a margin.

TIP

> **Open the Page Setup Dialog Box Using the Ruler**   Double-click any of the margins shown on the vertical or horizontal ruler. This opens the Page Setup dialog box.

To adjust a margin, place the mouse pointer between the gray margin and the white document area on the ruler. A margin-sizing arrow appears. Drag the gray margin to increase or decrease the respective margin. Figure 11.2 shows the margin-sizing arrow on the top margin on the vertical ruler.

Controlling Paper Types and Orientation

Other page attributes that you need to control in your documents are the paper size and the page orientation. Word's default settings assume that you will print to paper that is a standard 8.5×11 inches. The default page orientation is portrait, meaning that the maximum distance from the left edge to the right edge of the page is 8.5 inches.

You can select different paper sizes, which is particularly important if you want to print to envelopes or a different paper size. You can also change the orientation of your text and images as they appear on a page from portrait to landscape, where the page contents are rotated so that the distance between the left and right edges on a standard sheet of paper would be 11 inches.

Paper size and page orientation are both set in the Page Setup dialog box. Follow these steps to edit the settings for these page attributes:

1. Select **File**, **Page Setup**. The Page Setup dialog box opens.

2. Click the **Paper** tab on the dialog box (see Figure 11.3).

3. To select a new paper size, click the **Paper Size** drop-down box and select the paper type. For nonstandard paper sizes, select **Custom Size** in the **Page Size** box and then type the

paper's width into the **Width** box and its height into the **Height** box.

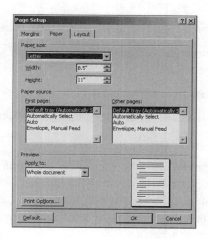

FIGURE 11.3
The Paper tab of the Page Setup dialog box enables you to set your paper size and source.

4. To change the orientation of the page to portrait or landscape, select the **Margins** tab and click the **Portrait** or the **Landscape** option button as needed (refer to Figure 11.1).

5. Finally, in the Apply To drop-down box, select **Whole Document** to apply the new settings to the new document or **This Point Forward** to apply the settings to the document from the current page forward.

6. When you complete editing the settings, click **OK**.

INSERTING PAGE BREAKS

As you create your document, Word automatically starts a new page when you fill the current page with text or other document items (such as graphics, tables, and so on). However, you can insert your own page breaks in the document as needed. These types of page breaks are often referred to as *hard*, or *manual*, page breaks.

To insert a page break into your document, follow these steps:

1. Place the insertion point in the document where you want to force a page break.

2. Select **Insert**, **Break**. The Break dialog box appears.

3. Make sure the Page Break option button is selected, and then click **OK**.

A page break is placed in your document. In the Normal view, the page break appears as a dashed line across the page, with "page break" denoted at the center of the line. In the Print Layout view, you can move to the new page by clicking the **Next Page** button on the bottom of the vertical scrollbar.

TIP

> **Use the Keyboard to Place a Page Break**   You can also place a page break in your document using the key-board. Hold down the **Ctrl** key, and then press the **Enter** key.

To remove a page break, switch to the Normal view (select **View**, **Normal**). The page break appears as a dotted line in the document and is denoted as a "page break." Select the page break with a mouse, and press **Delete** to remove it.

Changing Line Spacing

Another setting that greatly influences the amount of whitespace on the page is line spacing. When you consider whether you want your text single-spaced or double-spaced, those text attributes are con-trolled by changing the line spacing.

Line spacing can be set for each paragraph in the document or for selected text. Setting line spacing for a blank document allows you to set a default line spacing for all text paragraphs that will be placed in the document.

To set the line spacing for a new document, a paragraph, or selected text, follow these steps:

1. Select **Format, Paragraph**. The Paragraph dialog box appears (see Figure 11.4).

2. Make sure the **Indents and Spacing** tab on the dialog box is selected.

3. To change the line spacing, click the **Line Spacing** drop-down box and select one of the following choices:

   - **Single**—Spacing accommodates the largest font size found on the lines and adds a small amount of white-space (depending on the font used) between lines.

   - **1.5**—The line spacing is 1 and 1/2 times greater than single spacing.

   - **Double**—Twice the size of single line spacing.

   - **At Least**—(The default setting) Line spacing adjusts to accommodate the largest font on the line and special items, such as graphics.

   - **Exactly**—All lines are equally spaced, and special font sizes or items such as graphics are not accommodated. These items, if larger than the setting used here, appear cut off in the text. You can still accommodate these items by using the Multiple box.

   - **Multiple**—You specify the line spacing by a particular percentage. This feature is used in conjunction with the Exactly option to set a line spacing percentage that accommodates special font sizes or graphics found in the document. For example, if you want to decrease the line spacing by 20%, enter the number 0.8. To increase the line spacing by 50%, enter 1.5.

4. The **Line Spacing** option selected in step 3 is influenced by the point size entered in the **At** box (this applies only when you have selected At Least, Exactly, or Multiple). Use the click arrows to increase or decrease the point size of the line spacing, if needed.

TIP

Set Spacing Before and After a Paragraph   You can also set special spacing Before and After a particular paragraph. This is particularly useful for headings or other special text items.

5. When you complete setting the line spacing parameters, click **OK**.

If you find that you don't like the new line spacing settings for a particular paragraph, click the **Undo** button on the Standard toolbar to reverse the changes that you have made.

In this lesson, you learned to set margins for your documents, change the paper size and page orientation, and place page breaks in your documents. You also learned how to control line spacing in your paragraphs. In the next lesson, you will learn how to create and apply styles to the text in your documents.

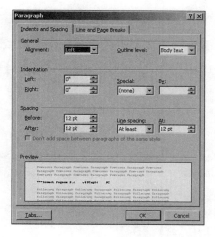

FIGURE 11.4
The Paragraph dialog box allows you to control the line spacing in your text.

Lesson 12
Working with Styles

In this lesson, you learn how to create text and paragraph styles. You also learn how to edit your styles and take advantage of the styles in the Style Gallery.

UNDERSTANDING STYLES

Word styles provide an excellent way to manage the character and paragraph formatting in a document. A *style* is a grouping of formatting attributes identified by a style name. You can create styles for text that contain character-formatting attributes such as bold, italic, or a particular font size; these types of styles are called *character styles*. You can also create styles for paragraphs that include paragraph attributes, such as alignment information, indents, and line spacing; this type of style is called a *paragraph style*.

You view the style names in the Styles and Formatting task pane (see Figure 12.1). To open the Styles and Formatting task pane, select the **Format** command and then click **Styles and Formatting**.

TIP

> **Select Styles and Formatting at the Touch of a Button**
> The easiest way to access the Styles and Formatting task pane is to use the **Styles and Formatting** button on the Formatting toolbar.

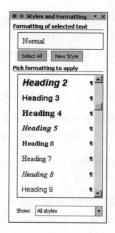

FIGURE 12.1
The Styles and Formatting task pane is the starting place for creating, editing, and managing the styles and formatting in your documents.

Word includes several built-in styles, such as the headings, that you can take advantage of in your documents. Styles are particularly useful because if you use them to format text or paragraphs in the document, you can change the attributes saved in the style at any time. These changes immediately take effect on all the text that has been assigned that style.

CAUTION

> **Paragraph Styles Versus Text Styles** Paragraph styles (the more commonly used option) assign both character and paragraph attributes to the paragraph containing the insertion point. Text styles affect only the word or words you select before you apply the style.

CREATING TEXT STYLES

Creating text styles is extremely easy. Select the text you want to emphasize with special character formatting and assign it all the character attributes (font type, bold, underline, italic, and so on) that you want to include in the style. You may assign the attributes using either the Font dialog box (by selecting **Format, Font**) or the appropriate buttons on the Formatting toolbar. Fonts are covered in Lesson 7, "Changing How Text Looks."

Make sure that the desired text is selected, and then follow these steps:

1. Select the **Styles and Formatting** task pane and then **New Style**; the New Style dialog box appears.

2. Click the **Style Type** drop-down box and select **Character** for the style type.

3. Look in the Formatting of Selected Text area of the Styles and Formatting task pane. Here you can see the text attributes that you have assigned to your selected text. Note that the new style is based on the current style (the default paragraph style or the normal style) plus your added attributes.

4. Type a name for your new style into the Name box.

5. Click **OK** to conclude the style creation process. You are returned to the Styles and Formatting task pane. Notice that your new style now appears in the Pick Formatting to Apply list in the task pane.

You can now assign the new character style to text in your document as needed. Simply select the text to which you want to assign this unique style, and then select the **Styles and Formatting** task pane. Select your unique style from the list provided. The style is applied to the selected text.

TIP

> **View All the Text Assigned a Particular Style**   If you would like to select all the different text items that you assigned a particular style, select the style in the Styles and Formatting task pane and then click the Select All button.

CREATING PARAGRAPH STYLES

Creating paragraph styles is similar to creating text styles. Apply to a paragraph the formatting that you want to include in the style (you can use alignment settings, indents, and all the paragraph attributes that you are familiar with). Make sure the insertion point is in the paragraph. You can create the style by following these steps:

1. Select the **Styles and Formatting** task pane and then **New Style**; the New Style dialog box appears.

2. Click the **Style Type** drop-down box and select **Paragraph** for the style type.

3. Type a unique name into the **Name** box for the style.

4. Click **OK** to return to the Styles and Formatting task pane. The style is now available on the Style list. You can now apply the style to any paragraph in the document by placing the insertion point in the paragraph.

EDITING STYLES

You can also edit or modify the attributes found in any of your styles or the default styles in the document. You edit styles using the Styles and Formatting task pane. Remember that when you edit a style, all the text to which the style was applied reflects the new text and paragraph attributes of your edited style.

To edit a style, follow these steps:

1. Select the **Styles and Formatting** task pane.

2. Under **Pick Formatting to Apply**, select the style you want to edit and place the mouse pointer on it until you see the box outline and down arrow appear. Then, click the down arrow and press **Modify**. The Modify Style dialog box appears as shown in Figure 12.2.

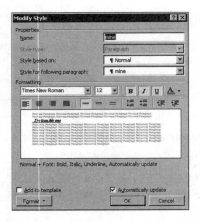

FIGURE 12.2
The Modify Style dialog box allows you to edit the name of a style and modify all the attributes found in the style.

3. To modify the style, select the **Format** button. A menu appears, allowing you to modify the following attributes in the style:

   - Font
   - Paragraph
   - Tabs

   - Borders
   - Language
   - Frame

   - Numbering

4. Select one of the choices provided in the Format box. The appropriate dialog box appears, allowing you to edit the settings for the chosen attributes. For example, if you want to modify the font attributes for the style, click the **Format** arrow and select **Font** from the list provided. The Font dialog box appears.

5. When you have finished modifying the Font attributes for the style (or for whichever style type you chose to modify), click **OK**. You are returned to the **Modify Style** dialog box.

6. Modify other attributes of the style as needed by making the appropriate choices from the menus.

7. When you have completed your style modifications, click
OK in the Modify Style dialog box and you return to the task
pane with the changes made.

TIP

> **You Can Delete Unwanted Styles**   You can delete styles
> that you've created that you no longer need. Open the
> **Styles and Formatting** task pane and place the mouse
> pointer on the style in the **Pick Formatting to Apply** list.
> Wait for the box outline and down arrow to appear, and
> then click the **Delete** button under the down arrow. The
> style is removed from the Style list.

USING THE STYLE ORGANIZER

Word also has the capability to copy styles from other documents and
templates into your current document. This provides you with an easy
way to add already existing styles to a document (rather than reinvent-
ing the wheel or style).

To copy styles from another document or template, follow these steps:

1. Select the **Tools** command, and then choose **Templates and
Add-Ins**.

2. In the Templates and Add-Ins dialog box, click the
Organizer button. The Organizer dialog box appears as
shown in Figure 12.3.

3. The styles in the current document appear on the left side of
the Organizer dialog box. Styles in the template that your
current document was based on are shown on the right side of
the Organizer dialog box (all documents are based on a template, even if it is just the Word Normal template). To close
the template file on the right side of the dialog box, click the
Close File button (in Figure 12.3, click **Close File** under the
Normal.dot template on the right of the dialog box).

4. Now you can open a new template or document and copy the styles that it contains to the current document (shown on the left of the dialog box). Click **Open File** on the right side of the Organizer dialog box. Locate the document or template from which you want to copy the styles. Double-click the file in the Open dialog box to open the file.

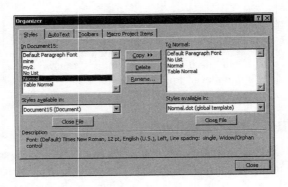

FIGURE 12.3
The Organizer dialog box makes it easy for you to copy a style or styles from one document to another.

5. You are returned to the Organizer dialog box, and the styles for the recently opened template or document are listed on the right side of the dialog box. To copy a style or styles, select the style and click the **Copy** button. The style is copied to the styles in your current document.

TIP

Copy More Than One Style at a Time   To select several styles to copy to your document simultaneously, click the first style you want to copy and then hold down the **Shift** key and click the last style you want to copy. All the styles in between these two are also selected. To select styles that are not in a series, click the first style you want to copy, and then hold down the **Ctrl** key and click any other styles you want to select.

6. When you have finished copying styles (styles can be copied from either of the documents in the Organizer dialog box), click **Close** to close the Organizer dialog box.

As you can see, the Organizer makes it very easy for you to share the styles that you create between your documents. Remember, styles that you create reside only in the document where you create them. The only way to copy those styles to another document is to use the Style Organizer.

In this lesson, you learned to create and assign character and paragraph styles. You also learned to modify your styles and learned how to copy styles from one document to another using the Organizer dialog box. In the next lesson, you will learn how to use AutoFormat to quickly change the way text and paragraphs look in your documents.

LESSON 13

Using AutoFormatting to Change Text Attributes

In this lesson, you learn how to quickly change the look of your text with AutoFormat and apply text attributes automatically as you type.

UNDERSTANDING AUTOFORMATTING

AutoFormat is a great feature that helps you create professional-looking documents. AutoFormatting actually examines the text elements that you have placed in your document (such as headings, tables, lists, regular body text, and other items) and then automatically formats these elements using an appropriate Word style. Even though this formatting is automatic, you can accept or reject the changes AutoFormatting makes. You can also make additional changes to the document as you see fit by using other styles or font and paragraph formatting attributes (for more about styles, see Lesson 12, "Working with Styles").

You will also find that AutoFormat does more than just apply styles to your document elements. It can remove extra line breaks between paragraphs and apply the hyperlink styles to e-mail addresses or Web addresses that you place in your documents.

You can use AutoFormat in two ways. You can turn on AutoFormatting so that items are formatted as you type, or you can create a new document and then use AutoFormat to format the entire document at once.

FORMATTING AS YOU TYPE

You can have your document elements formatted as you type. However, this feature requires that you supply Word with certain cues so that the correct formatting is applied to the text. For example, if you turn on AutoFormat As You Type and want to create a bulleted list that is automatically formatted by the AutoFormat feature, you must begin the bulleted line with a dash, an asterisk, or a lowercase "o" so that Word knows to apply the bulleted list formatting.

Many AutoFormat As You Type features are enabled by default; others are not. To customize the AutoFormat As You Type feature, follow these steps:

1. Select **Tools, AutoCorrect Options**. The AutoCorrect dialog box appears.

2. Select the **AutoFormat As You Type** tab on the dialog box (see Figure 13.1).

FIGURE 13.1

The AutoFormat As You Type tab of the AutoCorrect Options dialog box allows you to select which document elements will be formatted automatically as you type.

3. A series of check boxes on the AutoFormat As You Type tab allows you to select which document elements will be formatted as you type. Again, you need to type certain characters for a particular element so that the AutoFormat feature recognizes and then formats the text.

- **Built-In Heading Styles**—All headings that you apply to an outline or a legal document are automatically assigned the appropriate built-in heading style (using Headings 1–9).

- **Border Lines**—Borders are automatically placed between paragraphs. You must type three dashes (-) for a thin border, three underscores (_) for a bold line, or three equal signs (=) for a double-line border.

- **Tables**—Automatically creates tables. You must type a series of plus symbols (+) and dashes (-) to signify the number of columns (+) and the distance between the columns (-).

- **Automatic Bulleted Lists**—Creates bulleted lists automatically. Start each line in the list with an asterisk (*), a dash (-), or a lowercase "o."

- **Automatic Numbered Lists**—Creates numbered lists. Start a line with a letter or number and it is turned into a numbered list item. Paragraphs following the first numbered line are numbered sequentially if the Format Beginning of List Item Like the One Before It check box is selected.

Other AutoFormatting check boxes include features that format your quotation marks, ordinals (1st), and fractions (1/2). Select (or deselect) the various AutoFormat As You Type options and then click **OK** to close the dialog box.

TIP

Create Styles As You Type   If you select the Define Styles Based on Your Formatting check box, Word automatically takes your character and paragraph formatting attributes and turns them into styles. You can then use the created styles to format other paragraphs.

Although formatting as you type might seem like a real timesaver, you must remember which special characters to use to automatically begin a particular formatting type.

APPLYING AUTOFORMAT TO A DOCUMENT

The alternative to AutoFormatting as you type is to create the document and then format it after the fact with AutoFormat. Waiting to format a document until after its completion allows you to concentrate on the document content as you type. You then can concentrate on the look and feel of the document by selecting from the various AutoFormatting options. Heads, numbered or bulleted lists, and other items you have designated throughout the text are identified and formatted.

To AutoFormat a document, follow these steps:

1. Make sure that you are in the Print Layout view (select **View**, and then **Print Layout**—this allows you to see the various formatting tags applied to the document when you review the Autoformat changes). Select **Format, AutoFormat**. The AutoFormat dialog box appears (see Figure 13.2).

2. You can increase the accuracy of the formatting process by choosing a particular document type. Click the General Document type drop-down arrow and select from the document types listed on the drop-down list (the default setting is **General Document**; you can also select **Letter** or **Memo** as the document type from the list).

FIGURE 13.2
The AutoFormat dialog box allows you to immediately format the document or review each of the suggested formatting changes.

3. Now you can AutoFormat the document. If you want to AutoFormat the current document without reviewing the formatting changes, click the **AutoFormat Now** option button and then click **OK**. The document is automatically formatted.

4. If you want to review the AutoFormatting process after the changes are made, click the **AutoFormat and Review Each Change** option button. Then click **OK**.

5. The document is formatted and then the AutoFormat/Review Changes dialog box appears. If you already know whether you are happy with the results, choose to **Accept All** or **Reject All** using the appropriate button in the dialog box. You can also click **Review Changes** to review the changes to your document so that you can decide whether you're happy with the results on a change-by-change basis. The Review AutoFormat Changes dialog box appears (see Figure 13.3).

6. Click the **Find** (forward) button (this button has a right-pointing arrow) to begin the review process. Notice that all the changes that AutoFormat has made to the document are tagged with a red line and a description box in the document.

7. When you are asked to review a particular change (the change appears in the Changes box), either select **Reject** to reject the change or click the **Find** button to skip to the next

formatting change in the document. You can also choose to **Accept All** or **Reject All** using the appropriate button in the dialog box.

FIGURE 13.3
This dialog box enables you to review each of the formatting changes made in the document.

8. When you reach the bottom of the document, Word notifies you that it can start searching for changes at the top of the document. If you had the insertion point at the top of the document when you began the review process, click **Cancel**. Then, click **Cancel** to close the two subsequent dialog boxes as well.

To safeguard any automatic formatting changes that have been made, be sure to immediately save your document.

CHANGING AUTOFORMAT OPTIONS

You can customize certain options related to the AutoFormat feature. This dialog box can be reached by selecting the **Tools** menu and then **AutoCorrect**. Make sure that the **AutoFormat** tab is selected.

The options that you have control over on the AutoFormat tab are similar to those found on the AutoFormat As You Type tab. You can choose check boxes that automatically format headings, lists, and so on (see Figure 13.4).

You can also choose to have Word retain the style that you have already placed in the document (prior to running AutoFormat). Select the **Styles** check box to do so.

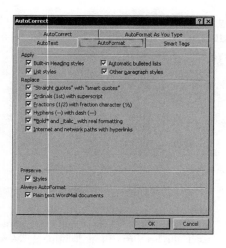

FIGURE 13.4
You can set the various options for automatic formatting on the AutoFormat tab of the AutoCorrect dialog box.

TIP

> **AutoFormat Text-Only E-mail Automatically** If you use Word as your e-mail editor for Outlook, you can have any text-only e-mail messages that you receive automatically formatted to look better when you read them. Select the **Plain Text Wordmail Document** check box at the bottom of the AutoFormat tab.

After you select the options you want to set for AutoFormat, select **OK**. You can now run AutoFormat and your options will be in force as your document is formatted.

In this lesson, you learned to AutoFormat your text as you typed and also to use AutoFormat to format a completed document. In the next lesson, you will learn how to use the AutoText feature and add special characters to your documents.

LESSON 14

Adding Document Text with AutoText and Using Special Characters

In this lesson, you learn how to quickly add repeating text elements to your documents using the AutoText feature. You also learn how to add special characters to your document, such as the copyright symbol.

UNDERSTANDING AUTOTEXT

AutoText provides you with a way to build a library of words and text phrases that you use often in your documents. An AutoText entry can consist of a company name, your name, or an entire paragraph that you commonly place in your documents.

AutoText makes it easy for you to quickly insert items from your AutoText list into any document. Creating AutoText entries is also very straightforward.

CREATING AUTOTEXT ENTRIES

You can create an AutoText entry using text from an existing document, or you can type the text that you want to add to the AutoText list in a blank document. It's then just a matter of copying the text to your AutoText list.

To create an AutoText entry, follow these steps:

1. Type the text you want to use for the AutoText entry or open the document containing the text that will serve as the AutoText entry.

2. Select the text.

3. Select the **Insert** menu, point at **AutoText**, and then select **New** from the cascading menu. The Create AutoText dialog box appears as shown in Figure 14.1.

 TIP

> **AutoText Isn't on My Insert Menu**   Remember that Word uses a personalized menu system that places your most recently used commands on the various menus. If you click a menu and don't see a particular command, rest your pointer in the menu for a moment; the menu will expand and provide a list of all the commands available on that particular menu.

FIGURE 14.1
Type a name for your new AutoText entry into the Create AutoText dialog box.

4. Type the name that you want to use to retrieve this AutoText entry in the text box provided (for one-word text entries, the selected text can also serve as the entry name).

5. After providing the name for the AutoText entry, click **OK**.

Your selected text is added to the AutoText list. You can repeat this procedure and add as many text items to the AutoText list as you want.

INSERTING AUTOTEXT ENTRIES

After you add an AutoText entry or entries to the list, you can insert them into any Word document. One method of inserting an AutoText entry into the current document is to pull the entry directly from the AutoText list.

To insert an AutoText entry into a document, follow these steps:

1. Place the insertion point in the document where you want to insert the AutoText entry.

2. Select the **Insert** menu, point at **AutoText**, and then select **AutoText**. The AutoCorrect dialog box appears as shown in Figure 14.2.

FIGURE 14.2
Insert your AutoText entries from the AutoCorrect dialog box.

3. The AutoText tab of the AutoCorrect dialog box displays an alphabetical list (as well as various default entries that Word provides) of the AutoText entries that you have added to the AutoText list. Select the entry you want to insert and click

Insert, or double-click any entry on the list to insert it into the document.

An alternative to manually inserting AutoText into the document is using the AutoComplete feature to automatically insert an entry into your document. For example, if you have an entry in your AutoText list that reads "I am pleased to announce," you can automatically insert this entry into your document by beginning to type the entry. As you type the first few letters in the AutoText entry, an AutoComplete box appears containing the complete AutoText entry, as shown in Figure 14.3.

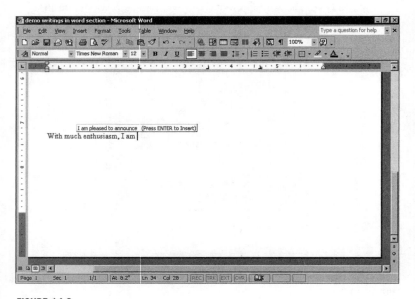

FIGURE 14.3

AutoComplete automatically places entries from your AutoText list into your documents.

To insert the entry into the document, press the **Enter** key. AutoComplete also helps you enter items that are not included on your AutoText list into your document. These items include the current date, days of the week, and names of months. For example, as you begin to type the name of a month, the AutoComplete box message appears telling you to press **Enter** to insert the complete word.

TIP

> **Use the AutoText Toolbar to Quickly Insert AutoText Entries**
> Right-click any toolbar and then select **AutoText** from the menu. To add an entry into the current document, click the **All Entries** button on the AutoText toolbar and select your AutoText from the list.

DELETING AUTOTEXT ENTRIES

You can easily delete items on the AutoText list when you no longer need them. This is done on the AutoText tab of the AutoCorrect dialog box.

To delete an AutoText entry, follow these steps:

1. Select the **Insert** menu, point at **AutoText**, and then select **AutoText** from the cascading menu. The AutoCorrect dialog box appears.

2. Select any of the entries in the AutoText list.

3. Click **Delete** to remove the entry from the list.

After you have completed your deletion of AutoText entries, click **OK** to close the AutoText dialog box.

USING SPECIAL CHARACTERS AND SYMBOLS

Special characters and symbols are characters that can't be found on your keyboard and that are not part of what is considered to be the standard character set. Characters such as the German "u" with an umlaut (Ü) are special characters, and an item such as the trademark is an example of a symbol.

Many special characters and symbols exist. Table 14.1 lists some of the commonly used special characters and symbols.

TABLE 14.1   Common Special Characters and Symbols

Special Character or Symbol	Use
Copyright symbol ©	Used in a copyright notice in a document.
Trademark symbol ™	Placed to the right of official trademarks in a document.
Em dash —	Used to bracket asides or sudden changes in emphasis in a sentence—rather than using a comma. It appears as a long dash.
En dash –	Slightly shorter than an em dash; this dash is commonly used to separate numbers from capital letters, such as Figure B–1.
Wingdings	A group of special icons that can be used in your documents for emphasis or as bullets.
Foreign language font (é)	Characters that include special accents.

The basic special characters and symbols are held in three groups:

- **Symbol**—This group contains mathematical symbols, arrows, trademark and copyright symbols, and letters from the Greek alphabet.

- **Normal Text**—This group provides you with characters containing accents and other special marks.

- **Wingdings**—Special icons and symbols for many purposes.

Additional special character sets might be available to you, depending on which fonts have been installed on your computer (you can purchase software with unique fonts and symbols, as well).

TIP

> **Shortcut to Making an Em Dash**   As you are typing, you may quickly insert an em dash into the text by pressing **Ctrl+Alt+**the minus sign on the number pad. The em dash appears.

You can easily insert special characters and symbols into your documents using the Insert Symbol feature. To insert a special character or symbol, follow these steps:

1. Place the insertion point in your document where you want to insert the special character or symbol. Select **Insert**, **Symbol**. The Symbol dialog box appears as shown in Figure 14.4.

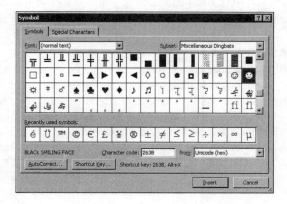

FIGURE 14.4
The Symbol dialog box gives you access to symbols and special characters that you can insert into your document.

2. To insert a symbol, make sure the Symbol tab is selected on the Insert dialog box (if you want to insert a special character, go to step 5). Use the Font drop-down box to select the symbol set from which you want to choose your symbol. The symbol set that you choose dictates which symbols are available, so select a symbol set that provides the symbol you

want to insert. You will find that the normal text symbol set provides most of the commonly used symbols, such as copyright and trademark.

3. After you select the symbol set (such as normal text, Symbol, Wingdings, or another font family), click to select the symbol you want to insert.

4. After selecting the symbol, click the **Insert** button.

5. If you want to insert a special character, such as the copyright symbol or an em dash, click the **Special Characters** tab on the Symbol dialog box.

6. Select the special character and then click **Insert**.

7. When you have finished inserting your symbol or special character, click the **Close** button on the Symbol dialog box.

After you've inserted the symbol or special character into the document, you can continue typing or editing your text. Symbols and special characters give your document a finished, typeset look.

In this lesson, you learned how to create an AutoText entry list and insert AutoText entries into your documents. You also learned to add special characters to your documents. In the next lesson, you will learn how to add headers, footers, and page numbers to your Word documents.

LESSON 15
Adding Headers, Footers, and Page Numbers

In this lesson, you learn how to add headers, footers, and page numbers to your documents.

UNDERSTANDING HEADERS AND FOOTERS

Another aspect of creating a document is using headers and footers to insert information that you want repeated on every page of the document or in the pages of a particular document section.

PLAIN ENGLISH

Header/Footer The header resides inside the top margin on the page; it holds information such as the date or draft number that appears at the top of every page of the document. Every section of a document could potentially have a separate header.

The footer resides inside the bottom margin of the page; it holds information such as the page number or other information that appears at the bottom of every page of the document. Every section of a document could potentially have a separate footer.

Headers and footers provide you with a way to include a document title, the current date, or the current page number on the top or bottom of each page in the document. Headers can include text, graphics, or other items.

ADDING HEADERS AND FOOTERS

You can add a header or footer to a document in any view. To add a header or footer, follow these steps:

1. Select **View, Header and Footer**. You are temporarily switched to the Print Layout mode and placed in the header area of the document (see Figure 15.1). The regular text area is dimmed and unavailable while you work in the header or footer box.

2. Type your text into the header area. If you want to create a footer, click the **Switch Between Header and Footer** button on the Header and Footer toolbar. The toolbar is also available in the document window.

3. You can add a page number, the current date, the current time, and other elements using the appropriate buttons on the Header and Footer toolbar (see Table 15.1).

4. In cases where you need to align or format the text, use the appropriate buttons on the Word Formatting toolbar (while in the header/footer areas) as you would for text on the document page.

5. When you have finished entering your header and footer text, click the **Close** button on the Header and Footer toolbar.

You are returned to your document text. In the Normal view, you are not able to see your header or footer. In the Print Layout view, however, header and footer text appears dimmed.

You can edit your headers and footers by selecting **View, Header and Footer**. Move to the appropriate header or footer using the navigation buttons on the Header and Footer toolbar, shown in Table 15.1. To quickly enter a header or footer box in the Print Layout view, double-click the header or footer text.

Header area   Header and Footer toolbar

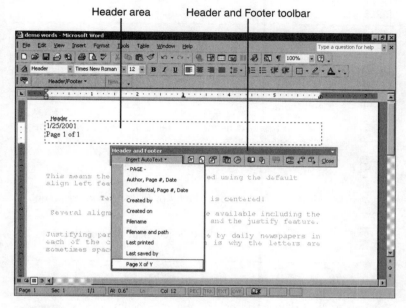

FIGURE 15.1
The header area of the page is where you type your header text. The Header and Footer toolbar provides you with tools to insert page numbers, insert the date, and to switch between your headers and footers.

TABLE 15.1   The Header and Footer Toolbar Buttons

Button	Purpose
	Inserts the page number
	Inserts the page count or number of total pages
	Edits the format of the page number
	Inserts the current date
	Inserts the current time

TABLE 15.1   (continued)

Button	Purpose
	Opens the Page Setup dialog box to the Layout tab, where you can change the header and footer settings
	Hides the document text while you work on your header and footer
	Sets up the next header the same as the current header (or footer)
	Switches between your header and footer
	Moves to the previous header or footer in the document
	Moves to the next header or footer in the document

Several toolbar choices, such as Same As Previous and Move to Previous or Next (header or footer), relate to documents that have several sections and so have different headers or footers within the same document. You can also have more than one header or footer in the document if you choose to have different headers or footers for odd- and even-numbered pages.

USING ODD- AND EVEN-NUMBERED PAGE HEADERS AND FOOTERS

By default, the header and footer layout settings in Word assume that one header or footer appears on all the pages of a document (except in cases where the document is divided into more than one section; each section can have different headers and footers). You can change the header and footer settings so that different headers and/or footers appear on the odd- and even-numbered pages of your document (or the odd- and even-numbered pages of a document section).

To change the layout settings for Word Headers and Footers, follow these steps:

1. After activating the Header and Footer view (so that the Header and Footer toolbar appears), click the **Page Setup** button.

2. In the Page Setup dialog box, click the **Different Odd and Even** check box to enable odd and even headers and/or footers in the current document (or document section).

TIP

> **Changing Header and Footer Layout When You Aren't in the Header or Footer**   To get to the header and footer layout options when you don't have the header or footer displayed, select **File**, **Page Setup**. The Page Setup dialog box appears. If it is not already selected, click the **Layout** tab.

3. If you want to have a header or footer (or none) on the first page of your document that is different from subsequent pages in the document, click the **Different First Page** check box (see Figure 15.2).

4. Click **OK** to close the Page Setup dialog box. If you are returned to your document, select **View**, **Header and Footer** to add the odd- or even-numbered page headers to the document otherwise you are returned to the current header and footer.

5. If you want to specify how close the header or footer is to the margin edge of the top or bottom of the document, respectively, use the Header or Footer spin boxes to set the distance.

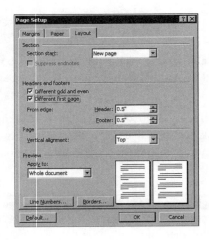

FIGURE 15.2
On the Layout tab of the Page Setup dialog box, you can select whether to have different odd- and even-numbered page headers/footers or a different header/footer on the first page of the document.

6. When you have finished adding your odd- and even-numbered page headers and/or footers or your first page and subsequent page headers, click the **Close** button on the Header and Footer toolbar.

Odd- and even-numbered page headers and footers are set up exactly the way you would typically set up a header or footer in the document. Use the **Show Next** or **Show Previous** button to move between the odd- and even-numbered page headers or footers and enter the text you want to appear on them.

ADDING PAGE NUMBERING TO A DOCUMENT

Headers and footers enable you to place repeating information in your documents, including the date, other important text, and most importantly—page numbers. When you want to place only page numbers on your document pages, you can forgo the Header and Footer command and quickly add page numbers using the Insert menu.

To place page numbers in your document, follow these steps:

1. Select **Insert**, **Page Numbers**. The Page Numbers dialog box appears (see Figure 15.3).

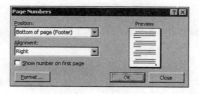

FIGURE 15.3
Use the Page Numbers dialog box to select the position and alignment of page numbers in your document.

2. To select the position for your page numbers, select the **Position** drop-down arrow and select **Top of Page (Header)** or **Bottom of Page (Footer)**.

3. You can select the alignment for the page numbers using the **Alignment** drop-down box. Select **Center**, **Left**, or **Right** to position the page numbers. When you are using mirror margins on a document that will be printed on both sides of the paper, select **Inside** or **Outside** (relative to a central binding—like that of a book) to position your page numbers.

4. To select the format for your page numbers, click the **Format** button. The Format dialog box appears.

5. Use the **Page Number Format** drop-down box (shown in Figure 15.4) to choose the format for your page numbers (Arabic numerals—1, 2, 3—is the default). When you have selected your number format, click **OK** to return to the Format dialog box.

FIGURE 15.4
Use the Page Number Format drop-down box to choose the format for your page numbers.

6. To have the page numbering start on a specific page in the document, click the **Start at** option button and then use the spinner box to specify the page number.

7. Click **OK** to close the Page Number Format dialog box.

The page numbers are placed in the header or footer of your document according to your positioning and formatting choices. You can edit the page numbers and add text if you want by selecting **View**, **Header and Footer**.

In this lesson, you learned to place headers and footers in your documents and you also learned how to add page numbering to your documents using the Insert menu. In the next lesson, you will learn how to print your documents and work with the various print options.

LESSON 16
Printing Documents

In this lesson, you learn how to preview your documents and then print them.

SENDING YOUR DOCUMENT TO THE PRINTER

When you have finished a particular document and are ready to generate a hard copy, Word gives you three choices. You can send the document directly to the printer by clicking the **Print** button on the Standard toolbar. You can open the Print dialog box (select **File**, **Print**) and set any print options that you want, such as printing a particular range of pages or printing multiple copies of the same document. You also have the option of previewing your hard copy before printing. This enables you to view your document exactly as it will appear on the printed page.

To preview your document before printing, click the **Print Preview** button on the Word Standard toolbar. The Print Preview window opens for the current document (see Figure 16.1).

You will find that the Print Preview window provides several viewing tools that you can use to examine your document before printing.

- **Zoom In or Out**—In the Print Preview window, the mouse pointer appears as a magnifying glass. Click once on your document to zoom in, and then click a second time to zoom out. To turn this feature off (or on again), click the **Magnifier** button.

- **Zoom by Percentage**—You can change to different zoom levels on the current document by using the **Zoom** drop-down arrow.

- **View Multiple Pages**—You can also zoom out and view several pages at once in the Preview window. Click **Multiple Pages**, and then drag to select the number of pages to be shown at once.

- **Shrink to Fit**—In cases where you have a two-page document and only a small amount of text appears on the second page, you can condense all the text to fit on the first page by clicking the **Shrink to Fit** button.

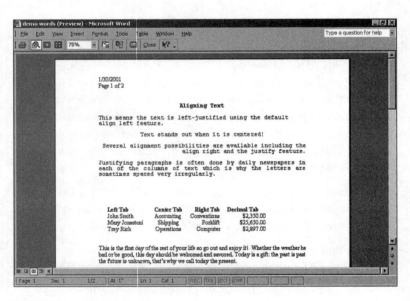

FIGURE 16.1
The Print Preview mode enables you to view your document the way it will print.

When you have completed viewing your document in the Print Preview mode, you can either click the **Print** button to print the document, or, if you want to edit the document before printing, click the **Close** button on the toolbar.

CHANGING PRINT SETTINGS

The Print dialog box supplies you with several options, including the printer to which you send the print job, the number of copies desired, and the page range to be printed.

To open the Print dialog box, select **File, Print**. The Print dialog box is shown in Figure 16.2.

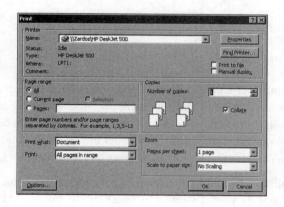

FIGURE 16.2
The Print dialog box gives you control over the various print options for your document.

Depending on your home or office situation, you might have your computer connected to more than one printer. The Print dialog box has a drop-down box that lists all the printers to which you have access. To select a printer other than the current printer, click the drop-down arrow in the **Name** box and choose your printer from the list.

The Print dialog box also enables you to select the range to be printed:

- **All Pages**—To print all the pages in the document, make sure the **All** option button is selected.

- **Current Page**—To print a single page, click the **Current Page** option button (this prints the page that the insertion point is parked on).

- **Page Range**—To designate a range of pages, click the **Pages** option button and type the page numbers into the Pages box.

TIP

> **Specifying Page Ranges**   To print a continuous range of pages, use the 1–5 format (where 1 is the start and 5 is the end of the range). For pages not in a continuous range, use the 5,9,11 format (where each distinct page number to be printed is separated by a comma). You can also mix the two formats. For example, you could specify 1–5,9,11.

- **Number of Copies**—In the Copies area of the Print dialog box, use the increment buttons in the Number of Copies box to select the number of copies you want to print. You can also double-click inside the Number of Copies box and type in a particular value for the number of copies you want.

- **Collate**—In addition to specifying the number of copies, you can collate your document by checking the Collate box in the copies area. *Collate* means that the document is printed in the proper order for stapling or binding.

You can also choose to print all the pages in a chosen range or print only the odd or even pages. Click the **Print** drop-down box (near the bottom left of the dialog box) and select **All Pages in Range**, **Odd Pages**, or **Even Pages**, as required.

Another print option worth mentioning is the Zoom print option in the Print dialog box. This feature enables you to place several document pages on one sheet of paper. To use Zoom print, click the **Pages per Sheet** drop-down box in the **Zoom** area of the Print dialog box and select the number of document pages you want to place on a sheet of paper. To select a scale for the print job (the scale is the relative size of the mini-pages on the printout page, such as 8.5 × 11 inches or legal size), click the **Scale to Paper Size** drop-down box.

After you select these two options, proceed with your print job. Be advised, however, that the more pages you place on a single sheet, the smaller the text appears.

Finally, you can print special items that you have placed in your document, such as comments, styles, and AutoText entries. When you choose to print one of these items, you are supplied with a page or pages separate from the main document that list the comments, styles, or other items you've selected.

Select the **Print What** drop-down arrow and select from the list of items (**Document**, **Document Properties**, **Document Showing Markup**, **List of Markup**, **Styles**, **AutoText Entries**, or **Key Assignments**). If you want to print more than one of these optional items with the document printout, you must select them in the Print Options dialog box.

SELECTING PAPER TRAYS, DRAFT QUALITY, AND OTHER OPTIONS

Several additional print options are also available from the Print dialog box. To access these options, click the **Options** button on the bottom left of the Print dialog box (see Figure 16.3).

The Print options dialog box gives you control over the output of the print job, as well as other options. You can also select the paper tray in your printer that you want to use for the print job (this is very useful in cases where you have a specific tray for letterhead, envelopes, and so on). Several of these options are described in Table 16.1.

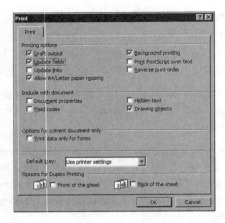

FIGURE 16.3
In the Print options dialog box, you can select or deselect certain options associated with your print job.

TABLE 16.1   Print Options on the Print Dialog Box

Option	Purpose
Draft Output	Prints the document faster with less resolution
Reverse Print Order	Prints pages last to first, collating your document on printers that output documents face up
Background Printing	Prints the document quickly to a memory buffer so that you can work while the output is actually sent out to the printer
Document Properties	Prints the document properties

When you have finished selecting the various options for printing your document, click the **OK** button. You are returned to the Print dialog box. When you are ready to print the document, click **OK**.

In this lesson, you learned how to preview and print your Word documents. In the next lesson, you will learn how to create bulleted and numbered lists.

LESSON 17
Creating Numbered and Bulleted Lists

In this lesson, you learn how to create and edit numbered and bulleted lists.

UNDERSTANDING NUMBERED AND BULLETED LISTS

You can add emphasis to a list of points or delineate a list of items in a document by adding numbers or bullets to the items in the list. Numbered lists are great for steps that should be read in order. Bulleted lists work best when you want to separate and highlight different items, but they do not have to appear in any order.

The style of the numbers or bullets that you apply to a list can easily be edited, and you can even change the starting number for a numbered list. The list then renumbers itself automatically. Also, as you add new lines to numbered or bulleted lists, the items are automatically set up with the same numbering style (with the proper number in the list sequence) or bullet style.

CREATING A NUMBERED OR A BULLETED LIST

You can create numbered or bulleted lists from scratch or add numbers or bullets to an existing list.

To create a new numbered list, follow these steps:

1. Place the insertion point where you want to begin the numbered list in your document.

2. Select **Format**, **Bullets and Numbering**. The Bullets and Numbering dialog box appears.

3. For a numbered list, select the **Numbered** tab (see Figure 17.1).

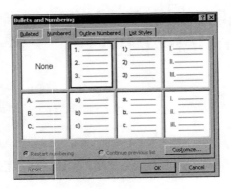

FIGURE 17.1
Use the Numbered tab on the Bullets and Numbering dialog box to select a number style for your numbered list.

TIP

> ☰ ☰ **Quickly Start a Numbered or Bulleted List**   To start a numbered or bulleted list using the default number or bullet style, click the **Numbering** or **Bullets** button on the Formatting toolbar. To turn off the numbers or bullets, click the appropriate button on the toolbar.

4. On the **Numbered** tab, click the style box for the style that you want to use. If you want to customize any of the default styles offered, select the style box and then click the **Customize** button. The Customize Numbered List dialog box appears (see Figure 17.2).

5. Use this dialog box to change the number style, the format, the start number, the font for the numbers, or the number position. A preview of your changes appears at the bottom of the dialog box.

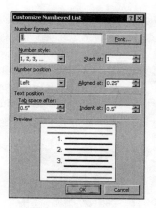

FIGURE 17.2
*The Customize Numbered List dialog box enables you to set the number style,
format, and start number for the list.*

6. When you have selected your options for the number style
for your list, click **OK**. You are returned to the Bullets and
Numbering dialog box. Click **OK** to return to the document.

You can also easily create a bulleted list using the Bullets and
Numbering dialog box; follow these steps:

1. To start a bulleted list, open the Bullets and Numbering dialog box, as previously discussed (select **Format**, **Bullets and
Numbering**). Click the **Bulleted** tab.

2. Select the bullet style you want to use by clicking the appropriate box. If you need to customize your bullet style, click
the **Customize** button (see Figure 17.3).

3. The Customize dialog box enables you to select any symbol
available in the various font symbol sets or create your button
from a graphic available in the Office clip art library. Use the

Font and **Character** buttons to select your bullet style from the various symbol sets (as discussed in Lesson 14, "Adding Document Text with AutoText and Using Special Characters"). If you want to use a graphic as the bullet, click the **Picture** button. Use the Picture Bullet dialog box that appears to select the bullet graphic you want to use, and then click **OK** (see Figure 17.4).

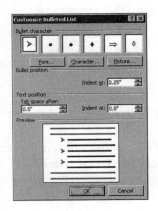

FIGURE 17.3
Use the Customize Bulleted List dialog box to select the bullet style or shape for your bulleted list.

4. Your new bullet style will appear in the Customize Bulleted List dialog box. Click **OK** to return to the Bullets and Numbering dialog box.

5. When you are ready to begin the bulleted list, click **OK** to close the Bullets and Numbering dialog box. The first bullet for the list will appear in your document.

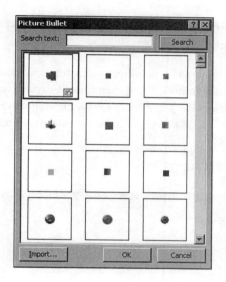

FIGURE 17.4
You can select from several bullet graphics using the Picture Bullet dialog box.

ADDING ITEMS TO THE LIST

After you've turned on numbering or bulleting, you will notice that a number or a bullet appears at the beginning of the line that holds the insertion point. Type the text for this numbered or bulleted item.

Press the **Enter** key to begin a new line. The numbering (sequentially) or bulleting continues with each subsequent line. Just add the needed text and press **Enter** whenever you are ready to move to the next new item in the list.

You can turn off the numbering or bulleting when you have finished creating your list. Click the **Numbering** button or the **Bullets** button, as appropriate, on the Formatting toolbar.

CREATING A NUMBERED OR A BULLETED LIST FROM EXISTING TEXT

You can also add numbers or bullets to existing text. Select the text list, as shown in Figure 17.5, and then select **Format, Bullets and Numbering**. Select the appropriate tab on the Bullets and Numbering dialog box and select the style of bullets or numbers you want to use.

When you have completed making your selection, click **OK**. The numbers or bullets appear on the text list.

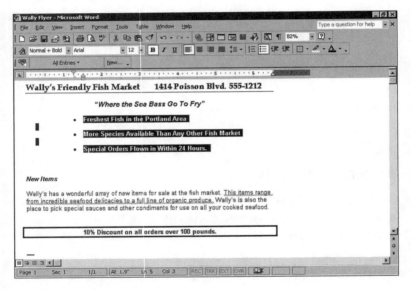

FIGURE 17.5
Select an existing text list and then add numbers or bullets to the list.

TIP

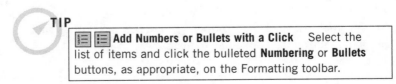

Add Numbers or Bullets with a Click   Select the list of items and click the bulleted **Numbering** or **Bullets** buttons, as appropriate, on the Formatting toolbar.

CREATING MULTILEVEL LISTS

You can also create multilevel lists by using the numbering and bullet feature. Multilevel lists contain two or more levels within a particular list. For example, a multilevel list might number primary items in the list, but secondary items (which fall under a particular primary item) in the list are denoted by sequential letters of the alphabet. Figure 17.6 shows a numbered, multilevel list.

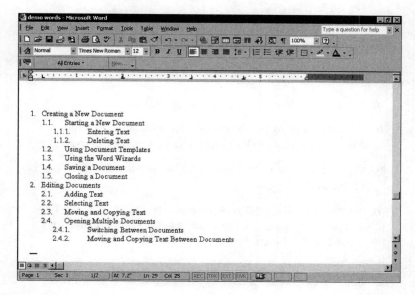

FIGURE 17.6
A multilevel numbered list uses several levels of numbering, as an outline does.

To create a multilevel list, follow these steps:

1. Place the insertion point where you want to begin the list or select text in an already existing list.

2. Select **Format**, **Bullets and Numbering**. The Bullets and Numbering dialog box opens.

3. Click the **Outline Numbered** tab to view the multilevel options (see Figure 17.7).

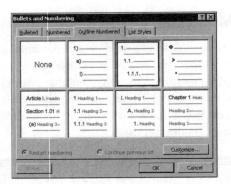

FIGURE 17.7
Use the Outline Numbered tabto select the outline style for your multilevel list.

4. Select the style of multilevel list for your document.

5. After customizing the list options in the Customize Outline Numbered list, click **OK** to return to the Outline Numbered tab.

6. Click **OK** to close the Bullets and Numbering dialog box and return to the document.

7. To enter first-level items in the list, type the item (it will be automatically numbered as is appropriate). Press **Enter** to move to the following line.

8. To demote the next line to the next sublevel (the next level of numbering), press the **Tab** key. Then, type your text. Press **Enter** to move to the following line.

9. If you decide to promote a line that you have demoted using the **Tab** key, be sure the insertion point is on that line, and then press **Shift+Tab**. When you have finished with the current line, press **Enter** to continue.

When you have completed your list, you can turn off the numbering by clicking the **Numbering** button on the Formatting toolbar.

 In this lesson, you learned how to create numbered, bulleted, and multilevel lists. In the next lesson, you will learn how to work with Word tables.

LESSON 18
Using Word Tables

In this lesson, you learn how to create and format tables in your Word document. You also learn how to place math formulas in a table.

UNDERSTANDING TABLES AND CELLS

A Word table is made up of vertical columns and horizontal rows—a tabular format. The intersection of a row and a column in a table is called a *cell*. A tabular format gives you flexibility to arrange text and graphics in an organized fashion. Tables enable you to enter and work with information in a self-contained grid.

Word makes it easy for you to create and edit a table of any size with any number of columns and rows. In addition to editing text or graphics in a table, you have access to several formatting options related to the table itself, such as row and column attributes and the capability to easily add or delete rows and columns from the table.

Word also offers you several approaches for actually placing the table into the document. You can insert the table into the document or draw the table using the Draw Table command.

INSERTING A TABLE

One option for placing a table into your document is inserting the table. Inserting a table enables you to select the number of rows and columns in the table. The height and width of the rows and columns are set to the default (one line space—based on the current font height—for the row height and 1.23 inches for the column width). Using the Insert command for a new table is the simplest way to select the number of rows and columns in the table. To place the table, you need only to place the insertion point at the position where the new table is to be inserted. The insertion point marks the top-left starting point of the table.

Inserted tables are static; you can move them to a new location in a document simply by selecting the entire table and then using cut and paste. If you want to have better control over the placement of the table, you might want to draw a table (as described in the next section). The drawn table can be dragged to any location in the document because it is created inside a portable frame.

To insert a table into your document, follow these steps:

1. Place the insertion point in the document where you want to place the table; select **Table**, and then point to **Insert**. Select **Table** from the cascading menu. The Insert Table dialog box appears (see Figure 18.1).

FIGURE 18.1
The Insert Table dialog box enables you to specify the number of columns and rows in your new table.

2. Use the click arrows in the **Number of Columns** text box to set the number of columns. Use the click arrows in the **Number of Rows** text box to set the number of rows.

3. If you want to set the number of columns and rows as the default for subsequent tables, click the **Set As Default for New Tables** check box.

4. To set the table so that it automatically adjusts the column widths to accommodate the text that you type in the column, select the **AutoFit to Contents** option button. If you are going to save the Word document containing the table as a Web document (and use it on a Web site), select the **AutoFit to Window** option button. This allows the table to automatically adjust within a Web browser window so that it can be viewed when the browser window is sized.

5. When you have completed your settings for the table, click **OK**.

The table is inserted into your document.

TIP

 Use the Toolbar to Insert a Table   Click the **Insert Table** button on the Standard toolbar, and then drag down and to the right to select the number of rows and columns (a column and row counter shows you the number selected). Release the mouse to insert the table (or click cancel if you change your mind).

DRAWING A TABLE

An alternative to inserting a table into your document is to draw the table. This method creates a table that resides inside a table cell. (This cell is not the same thing as the intersection of a column and a row, but a movable box that the table lives inside—much like a frame. It can be dragged to any position in the document.) You actually draw the table with a drawing tool and use the tool to add rows and columns to the table.

When you draw the table, you will find that it is created without any rows or columns. You then must manually insert the rows and columns using the Table Drawing tool. Although you can build a highly customized table using this method, it is not as fast as inserting a table with a prescribed number of rows and columns, as described in the previous section.

To draw a table in your document, follow these steps:

1. Select **Table**, **Draw Table**. The mouse pointer becomes a "pencil" drawing tool. The Tables and Borders toolbar also appears in the document window.

2. Click and drag to create the table's outside borders (its box shape). Release the mouse when you have the outside perimeter of the table completed.

3. To add rows and columns to the table, use the pencil to draw (hold down the left mouse button and drag the mouse) the row and column lines (see Figure 18.2).

4. When you have completed your table, click the **Tables and Borders** button on the standard toolbar to deactivate the Draw Tables feature.

TIP

> **Use the Tables and Borders Button to Show Draw Tables Tools**   Click the **Tables and Borders** button on the Standard toolbar, and the Draw Table pencil pointer appears on your screen. Click the button again when you are finished drawing.

The Tables and Borders toolbar provides you with buttons that enable you to edit the attributes of the table. Several of the buttons on the Tables and Borders toolbar are useful for customizing your table:

- **Distribute Rows Evenly**—Makes the row heights in the table consistent.

- **Distribute Columns Evenly**—Makes all the column widths consistent.

- **Eraser**—Enables you to turn on the eraser; drag the eraser across any row or column line in the table to erase it.

- **Line Style**—Enables you to change the weight and style of the row or column lines you create.

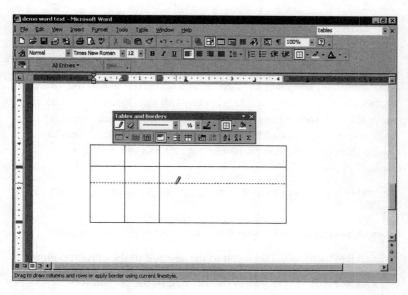

FIGURE 18.2
With the table drawing tool, you can draw a table in your document, and then draw in the row and column lines. The borders all snap to right-angled lines on an unseen grid so your table will always have straight lines.

You can also move the table anywhere on the document page (it's not anchored in one place like tables that are placed on the page using the Insert Table command). Place the mouse on the upper-left edge of the table and a Move icon (a four-headed arrow) appears. Drag the icon to a new location on the page. When you release the mouse, the table is placed in the new location.

CAUTION

When I Insert or Draw a Table, My Screen View Changes
For you to be able to see the table formatting as it occurs, Word automatically sets your document view to Print Layout. If you had previously been in the Normal view, your screen will look different because it is now showing all layout instructions. To switch back, select your desired page view under the **View** menu.

ENTERING TEXT AND NAVIGATING IN A TABLE

Entering text into the table is very straightforward. Click in the first cell of the table (the open box where the first column and first row of the table meet) and enter the appropriate text. To move to the next cell (horizontally, then vertically), press the **Tab** key. You can continue to move through the cells in the tables by pressing **Tab** and entering your text. If you want to back up a cell, press **Shift+Tab**. This moves you to the cell to the left of the current cell and selects any text entered in that cell.

Several other keyboard combinations are useful as you work in your table:

- **Alt+Home**—Takes you to the first cell in the current row
- **Alt+Page Up**—Takes you to the top cell in the current column
- **Alt+End**—Takes you to the last cell in the current row
- **Alt+Page Down**—Takes you to the last cell in the current column

Of course, you can use the mouse to click any cell of the table at any time.

Deleting text in the table is really no different from deleting text in your document. Select text in the table and press **Delete** to remove it. If you want to delete text in an entire row, but you want to keep the row in the table, place the mouse pointer at the left edge of the particular row. The mouse arrow pointer appears in the selection area. Click to select the entire row. When you press Delete, all the text in the cells in that particular row is deleted. You can also use a column pointer (a solid black arrow; place the mouse at the top of any column) to select an entire column and delete text using the Delete key.

INSERTING AND DELETING ROWS AND COLUMNS

You also have complete control over the number of rows and columns in your table. You can delete empty or filled rows and columns depending on your particular need.

To insert a row or column into the table, place the insertion point in a cell that is in the row or column next to where you want to place a new row or column. Select **Table** and then point to **Insert** to see the available options. Options can be selected from a cascading menu:

- **Rows Above**—Insert a new row above the selected row.

- **Rows Below**—Insert a new row below the selected row.

- **Columns to the Left**—Insert a new column to the left of the selected column.

- **Columns to the Right**—Insert a new column to the right of the selected column.

You can also easily delete columns or rows from your table. Select the rows or columns, and then select the **Table** menu. Point at **Delete**, and then select **Columns** or **Rows** from the cascading menu, as appropriate. The columns or rows selected are removed from the table.

TIP

Quick Select Multiple Columns   To select several cells, drag the mouse across them. You can also click the first cell in the series and then hold down the **Shift** key as you click the last cell you want to select.

FORMATTING A TABLE

Formatting a table can involve several things—you can change the width of a column or the height of a row and can also format the various table borders with different line weights or colors. Some of the table attributes can be modified directly on the table, but other attributes are best handled by modifying settings in the Table Properties dialog box or by using the AutoFormat dialog box.

MODIFYING CELL SIZE

An important aspect of working with your rows and columns is adjusting column widths and row heights to fit the needs of the information that you place inside the table cells. Both of these formatting tasks are mouse work. However, in cases where you want to enter an actual value for all the column widths or row heights, you can use the Table Properties dialog box discussed in this section.

Place the mouse pointer on the border between any columns in your table. A sizing tool appears (see Figure 18.3). Drag the sizing tool to adjust the width of the column.

TIP

> **Use the Ruler As Your Guide**   You can also use the column border markers on the ruler to adjust the width of a column or columns in your table. This provides a method of sizing columns using the ruler as a measurement guide. Drag the marker on the ruler to the appropriate width. To view the ruler, select **View, Ruler**.

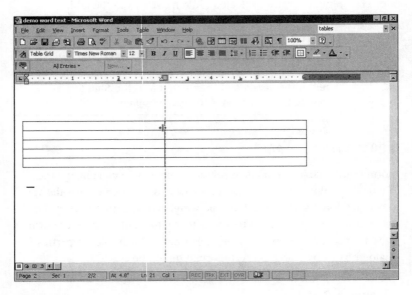

FIGURE 18.3
Use the column sizing tool to adjust the width of a column.

CAUTION

Be Careful When Sizing Columns If a Cell Is Selected   If a cell is selected anywhere in a column and you attempt to drag the sizing tool to change the column width, only the width of the row holding the selected cell is changed. Make sure no cells are selected if you want to size the entire column.

You can also adjust the column widths and the row heights in the table using the Table Properties dialog box. If you want to adjust the row or column attributes for just one row or column, make sure the insertion point is in that row or column. If you want to adjust the values for the entire table, click anywhere in the table, choose the **Table** menu, point at **Select**, and then choose **Table**. This selects the entire table.

Follow these steps to open the dialog box and adjust the various properties associated with the current table:

1. Select **Table**, **Table Properties**. The Table Properties dialog box appears.

2. To adjust column widths using the dialog box, select the **Column** tab.

3. Make sure the **Specify Width** check box is selected, and then use the width click arrows to adjust the width (see Figure 18.4).

4. If you want to change the width of the next column, click the **Next Column** button. The **Previous Column** button enables you to adjust the width of the previous column.

5. When you have completed adjusting column widths, click the **OK** button.

You can adjust row heights in a like manner. Use the **Row** tab of the Table Properties dialog box. You can use the Specify Height box to specify the row height and Previous Row and Next Row buttons to specify the row for which you want to adjust the height.

FIGURE 18.4
Adjust your column widths using the Column tab of the Table Properties dialog box.

TIP

> **Working with Drawn Tables**   If you've created your table using the Draw Table command and then inserted your rows and columns with the Drawing tool, you might find it faster to align any irregularly sized elements (such as rows or columns) with the mouse rather than using the Table Properties dialog box.

Formatting Table Borders

Formatting your table borders is a matter of selecting the cells (or the entire table) and then selecting the formatting parameters. After you've selected the appropriate cells, select the **Format** menu, and then select **Borders and Shading**.

TIP

> **Select the Entire Table**   A fast way to select the entire table is to place the insertion point in the table and then select **Table**, point at **Select**, and select **Table** again.

The Borders and Shading dialog box appears. Select the style of border that you want to place on the selected area of the table.

To select the border style, choose from one of the following:

- **Box**—This places a box around the outside of the table.

- **All**—This places a box around the table, gridlines inside the table, and also applies any shadow and color parameters that have been set in Word.

- **Grid**—This places a border around the table and places a border (grid) on the row and column lines.

- **Custom**—To change the style, color, and width of your border lines, use the **Style**, **Color**, and **Width** drop-down boxes to select the options for your border lines. When you have completed your selections, click **OK** to return to the table.

The border options that you selected are used to format the cells that you selected in the table.

AUTOMATICALLY FORMATTING THE TABLE

You can also format your table in a more automatic fashion using the Table AutoFormat feature. This feature enables you to select from a list of predetermined table formats that configure the borders and provide text and background colors in the cells. You can even select a particular font for the text contained in the cells.

To AutoFormat your table, click any cell of the table and then follow these steps:

1. Select **Table**, **AutoFormat**. The Table AutoFormat dialog box appears (see Figure 18.5).

2. To preview the various formats provided, click a format in the **Formats** scroll box. A preview of the format is shown.

3. When you have found the format that you want to use, select the format and then click **Apply**.

TIP

Select the Table Items You Want to Format with AutoFormat
The AutoFormat dialog box provides several check boxes (Borders, Shading, Font, Color, and so on) that can be deselected if you don't want your AutoFormat selection to format these particular items in your table.

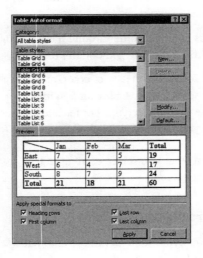

FIGURE 18.5
The Table AutoFormat dialog box enables you to select and apply a format style for your entire table.

In this lesson, you learned how to create, edit, and format tables. In the next lesson, you will learn how to create columns in your documents.

LESSON 19

Creating Columns in a Document

In this lesson, you learn how to create and edit column settings in your document.

UNDERSTANDING WORD COLUMNS

Word makes it very easy for you to insert and format columns for newsletters, brochures, and other special documents. It gives you complete control over the number of columns, column widths, and the space between the columns. You can insert columns for the entire page run of a document or place columns only in a particular document section.

The columns that you work with in Word are called newspaper or "snaking columns." This means that if you have two columns on a page and fill the first column, the text snakes over into the second column and continues there. This format is typical of your daily newspaper's columns.

TIP

For Side-by-Side Columns, Use a Table If you want to create columns that allow you to place paragraphs of information side by side in a document, place the text in a table that is not formatted with a visible border. This gives you great control over the individual text blocks in the separate columns that you create (see Lesson 18, "Using Word Tables").

CREATING COLUMNS

You can format a new document for columns, or you can select text and then apply column settings to that specific text. When you apply column settings to any selected text, Word automatically places the text (now in the number of columns you selected) into its own document section with a section break above and below the text. This allows you to switch from text in regular paragraphs (which are basically one column that covers all the space between the left and right margins) to text placed in multiple columns. You can also turn off the columns and return to text in paragraphs with very little effort on your part. Figure 19.1 shows a document that contains a section of text in paragraphs, followed by text in columns, and again followed by text in paragraphs (three sections in the same document). Sections are covered in Lesson 21, "Working with Larger Documents."

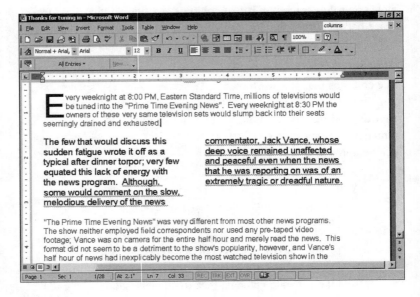

FIGURE 19.1

Documents can contain text in paragraphs and text in columns, as needed.

To place additional columns into a document, follow these steps:

1. Place the insertion point where you want the columns to begin or select the text that you want to format with the columns.

2. Select **Format**, **Columns**. The Columns dialog box appears (see Figure 19.2).

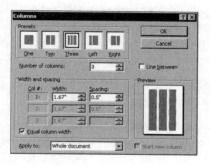

FIGURE 19.2
The Columns dialog box enables you to set the number of columns and column options for those that you place into your document.

3. To select the number of columns you want to place in the document, you can choose from several preset options or specify a number of custom columns. To use the presets select one of the following (all presets create columns separated by half-inch space):

   - **One**—The default setting; this removes columns from the document and places all text in the normal one-column configuration.

   - **Two**—Creates two equal columns.

   - **Three**—Creates three equal columns.

- **Left**—Creates two columns where the left column is half as wide as the right column.

- **Right**—Creates two columns where the right column is half as wide as the left column.

4. If you want to select a custom number of columns (rather than using the Presets), use the **Number of Columns** spinner box (or type a number in the box). Use the Width and Spacing box, located beneath the Number of Columns spinner box, to specify the width for each column and the distance between each of the columns.

5. If you want to place a vertical line between the columns, select the **Line Between** check box.

6. You can apply these new columns to the entire document (if you've selected text, it applies only to that particular text) or click the **Apply To** drop-down box and select **Whole Document** or **This Point Forward**. If you choose This Point Forward, the columns are placed in the document from the insertion point to the end of the document (in their own section).

7. When you have finished selecting your column options, click **OK**.

TIP

> ▦ **Create Columns with a Click of the Mouse** You can also create columns for currently selected text or insert columns into the text using the Columns button on the Standard toolbar. Click the **Columns** button and then select 1, 2, 3, or 4 columns from the drop-down box (you can choose **Cancel** if you change your mind). If you choose to create multiple columns using this method, columns of equal width are created.

Editing Column Settings

If you want to edit any of the column settings in your document, such as column number or column width, you can return to the Column dialog box to change any of the options.

1. Make sure that you click in the document section that contains the columns you want to modify.

2. Select **Format**, **Columns**. The Column dialog box appears.

3. Edit the various settings, described in the "Creating Columns" section, as needed. When you have completed your selections, click **OK**.

Inserting a Column Break

Because you are working with continuous, newspaper-type column settings, you might want to force a column break in a column. This allows you to balance the text between columns or end the text in a column at a particular point and force the rest of the text into the next column. To force a column break, follow these steps:

1. Place the insertion point in the column text where you want to force the break.

2. Select **Insert**, **Break**. The Break dialog box appears.

3. Select the **Column Break** option button.

4. Click **OK** to place the break in the column.

TIP

> **Use the Keyboard to Insert a Column Break**   You can also quickly place a column break in a column by pressing **Ctrl+Shift+Enter**.

The text at the break is moved into the next column in the document. Column breaks in the Print Layout view appear the way they will print, and all the column borders show in this view. In the Normal view, multiple columns are displayed as a single continuous column. The column break appears as a dotted horizontal line labeled Column Break.

REMOVING COLUMN BREAKS

Removing column breaks is very straightforward. Methods do vary, however, depending on the view that you are currently in.

In Print Layout mode, place the insertion point at the beginning of the text just after the break, click **Columns**, and then drag to select one column. This removes the break from the document.

 TIP

> ¶ **Use the Show/Hide Button to Reveal Column Breaks**
> You can also quickly show all your column breaks by clicking the **Show/Hide Button.** After you see the column breaks, just delete them.

In the Normal view, you can actually see the Column Break line (it appears as a dashed line). Select the break line with the mouse and then press **Delete**.

In this lesson, you learned to create and edit column settings in your documents. In the next lesson, you will learn to add graphics to your documents.

LESSON 20
Adding Graphics to a Document

In this lesson, you learn how to insert graphics, such as clip art, into your document and how to use the Word drawing tools to create your own graphics.

INSERTING A GRAPHIC

Adding a graphic to your document is really just a matter of identifying the place in the document where you want to place the picture and then selecting a specific graphic file. Word provides you with a large clip art gallery of ready-made graphics (in the metafile format .wmf). You can also place images into your document that you find on the Web, that you receive in to e-mail messages, that are imported from a scanner or digital camera, and more.

Word also embraces several graphic file formats, including the following file types:

- CompuServe GIF (.gif)
- Encapsulated PostScript (.eps)
- Various paint programs (.pcx)
- Tagged Image File format (.tif)
- Windows bitmap (.bmp)
- JPEG file interchange format (.jpg)
- WordPerfect graphics (.wpg)

To add a graphic file (a picture other than one of the Word clip art files), insert the image using the Insert menu.

Follow these steps to add a graphic to your document:

1. Place the insertion point where you want to place the graphic in the document.

2. Select **Insert, Picture,** and then select **From File** on the cascading menu. The Insert Picture dialog box appears.

3. Use the **Look In** box to locate the drive and folder that contains the picture file. After you locate the picture, click the file to view a preview (see Figure 20.1).

The Views drop-down arrow enables you to choose to see a list, preview, or thumbnails, among others.

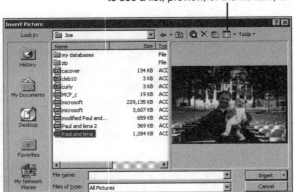

FIGURE 20.1
You can preview your graphical images before inserting them into your document.

4. After you select the picture you want to insert into the document, click **Insert** in the lower-right corner of the Insert Picture dialog box.

The picture is placed in your document and the Picture toolbar appears in the document window. The Picture toolbar provides several tools you can use to modify and edit the graphics in your document. See the "Modifying Graphics" section in this lesson.

Probably the first thing you will want to do to any graphic or picture that you insert into a document is size the image so it fits better on the page in relation to your text. Most inserted graphics, even those from the Office clip art library, tend to be inserted into a document in a fairly large size.

To size a graphic, click it to select it. Sizing handles (small boxes) appear on the border of the graphic. Place the mouse on any of these sizing handles. The mouse pointer becomes a sizing tool with arrows pointing in the directions in which you can change the size; drag to size the graphic. To maintain the height/width ratio of the image (so you don't stretch or distort the image), use the sizing handles on the corners of the image and drag diagonally.

TIP

Add a Graphic with Copy and Paste   You can copy a graphic to the Windows Clipboard from any Windows graphic program that you are running and then paste it into your Word document.

USING THE WORD CLIP ART

If you don't have a collection of your own pictures and graphics to place in your document, don't worry; Word provides a large collection of clip art images you can use to liven up your documents. The clip art library is organized by theme. For example, if you want to peruse the animal clip art that Word provides, select the **Animal** theme.

To insert Word clip art into your document, follow these steps:

1. Place the insertion point where you want to place the graphic in the document.

2. Select **Insert, Picture**, and then select **Clip Art** on the cascading menu. The Insert Clip Art task pane appears (see Figure 20.2).

FIGURE 20.2
The Insert Clip Art task pane gives you access to the Word clip art gallery.

3. Type in a clip art theme, such as **Animals**, into the **Search Text** area.

4. (Optional) By default, the search will be conducted on all your media collections, including the Office Collections. If you want to preclude certain collections from the search (to speed up the search process), click the **All Collections** drop-down arrow and clear the check mark from any of the locations listed.

5. (Optional) If you want to preclude certain file types from the search (to speed up the search process), select the **All Media File Types** drop-down box and deselect any of the file types (ClipArt, Photographs, and so on) as required.

TIP

> **Sound and Action Imagery Available, Too**   You can insert sound or movie clips into your document from the Clip Art task pane. By default, they are included in the results for any search you conduct.

6. Click the **Search** button and various clip art images that fit your search criteria appear.

7. When you have located the clip art you want to place in the document, click the image. An image drop-down box appears. Select **Insert** to place the image in your document (see Figure 20.3).

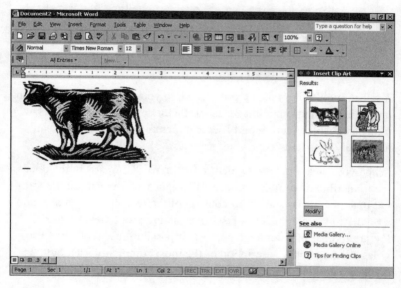

FIGURE 20.3
Click a particular clip art category to view the clip art images.

If used appropriately, pictures and clip art can definitely improve the look and feel of your documents—particularly special documents such as flyers, newsletters, and brochures. If you find the clip art library provided doesn't have what you need, click the **Media Gallery Online** link under the **See Also** section near the bottom of the task pane. Your Web browser opens and you go to Microsoft's online clip art library, which offers additional clip art images for your use.

CAUTION

Images and Copyright   Clip art images, such as those that ship with Microsoft Word, are considered "free" images and can be used in any of your Word documents. Other images that you find on the Web might be copyrighted. You are responsible for determining whether you have the right to use an image before copying it. Sometimes you can pay a fee for one-time use or make another agreement.

MODIFYING GRAPHICS

You can modify the images you place into your documents. An invaluable tool for modifying images is the Picture toolbar. It provides buttons that enable you to modify several picture parameters. You can also easily crop and resize your graphics.

When you click a picture (a picture file or Word clip art) in the document, the Picture toolbar automatically appears. You can use the toolbar to adjust the brightness or contrast of the image. You can also add a border to the graphic or adjust other picture properties. Word's Picture toolbar offers a large number of possibilities. Table 20.1 provides a listing and a description of the most commonly used buttons on the Picture toolbar.

TABLE 20.1   The Picture Toolbar Buttons and Their Purposes

Button	Click To
	Insert a new picture at the current picture position.
	Change the image to grayscale or black and white.
	Crop the image (after selecting, you must drag the image border to a new cropping position).
	Select a line style for the image border (you must first use the Borders and Shading command to add a border to the image).

TABLE 20.1 (continued)

Button	Click To
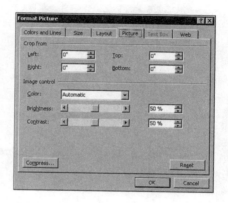 (icon)	Control how text wraps around the image (square, tight, behind image, and so on).
(icon)	Open the Format Picture dialog box.
(icon)	Reset the image to its original formatting values.

You can select from several formatting options for your picture when you select the **Format Picture** button; this opens the Format Picture dialog box (see Figure 20.4).

FIGURE 20.4
The Format Picture dialog box offers several ways to modify your picture.

The Format Picture dialog box provides several tabs that can be used to control various formatting attributes related to the picture. These tabs are

- **Colors and Lines**—Enables you to change the fill color (or background color) for the picture. This tab also provides settings for line weight and color and the style of arrows used

on lines. Line options are available only if you have created
the image using the tools on the Drawing toolbar.

- **Size**—Enables you to specify the height and width of the
  image in inches. It also enables you to specify the height and
  width scale (in percentages) for the image.

- **Layout**—Enables you to specify how text should wrap
  around the image (see Figure 20.5). Other options enable you
  to place the image behind or in front of the text.

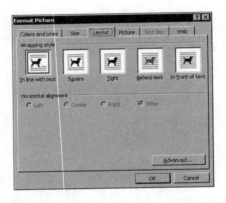

FIGURE 20.5
*The Layout tab of the Format Picture dialog box enables you to select how text
near the image is wrapped.*

- **Picture**—Enables you to crop the picture (refer to Figure
  20.4). It also provides an Image control area that lets you
  control the brightness and contrast of the image. You also can
  change the color of the image from the default (Automatic)
  to Grayscale, Black and White, or Washout using the Color
  drop-down box.

- **Web**—Enables you to include message text for the image
  that will appear as the image is loaded on a Web page. You
  need to use this option only if the Word document is going to
  be saved as a Web page for Web site.

CAUTION

> **Why Is the Text Box Tab Unavailable?**   The Text box tab is available only when you are using the dialog box to change the format options on a text box that you have created using the Text Box tool on the Drawing toolbar.

After making formatting changes to the picture using the Format Picture dialog box, click **OK** to return to your document.

TIP

> **Formatting Drawings You Create**   If you create your own image in a Word document using the tools on the Drawing toolbar, you can format the drawing using the Format Drawing Canvas dialog box that contains the same tabs as those found on the Format Picture dialog box. To open the Format Drawing Canvas dialog box, select the drawing you have created, and select **Format, Drawing Canvas**.

TIP

> **Resize or Crop with the Mouse**   Select the picture, and then drag the resizing handles (the black boxes on the picture borders) to increase or decrease the size. If you want to crop the picture, hold down the **Shift** key as you drag any of the resizing handles.

You can delete a picture you no longer want in the document by clicking the picture and then pressing **Delete**. You can also move or copy the picture using the **Cut, Copy, Paste** commands (for general information about moving, copying, and pasting items in Word, see Lesson 4, "Editing Documents").

Using the Word Drawing Toolbar

You can also create your own graphics in your documents using the drawing tools provided on the Word Drawing toolbar. This toolbar provides several tools, including line, arrow, rectangle, oval, and text box tools. You can also use the appropriate tools to change the fill color on a box or circle, change the line color on your drawing object, or change the arrow style on arrows you have placed on the page.

To display the Drawing toolbar, select **View**, point at **Toolbar**, and then select **Drawing** from the toolbar list.

 TIP

Quickly Access Toolbars You can also right-click any toolbar in the Word window to access the toolbar list; to choose the Drawing toolbar, select **Drawing**.

The Drawing toolbar appears at the bottom of the document window just above the Word status bar. Figure 20.6 shows the Drawing toolbar and the tools available on it.

 Word provides you with an add-on program called WordArt that enables you to create special text effects in your document. You can create text that wraps around a circle, as well as a number of other special text "looks." In Word, click the **WordArt** button on the Drawing toolbar to start the WordArt program. WordArt can also be used in other Office programs, such as PowerPoint, to create visually exciting text items.

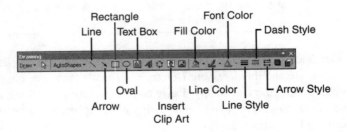

FIGURE 20.6
The Drawing toolbar makes it easy for you to create your own graphics in your documents.

CREATING A NEW OBJECT

To draw a particular object, click the appropriate button on the toolbar. Then, drag the mouse to create the object in your document. To draw a square or circle, click the **Rectangle** tool or the **Oval** tool and hold down the **Shift** key as you draw the object with the mouse. If you find that you aren't very good at actually drawing graphical objects, click the **AutoShapes** drop-down arrow (near the left side of the Drawing toolbar) and select a particular object shape from the list provided.

MODIFYING DRAWN OBJECTS

You can also control the various attributes for a particular object that you've drawn. You must first select the object using the selection pointer (click the **Select Objects** tool and then click the object). You can manipulate the object's line style, fill color, and line color. Just choose the appropriate tool on the toolbar and make your selection from the list of possibilities.

You can also size and move objects that you draw. Select an object and use the sizing handles to increase or decrease the size of the particular object. If you want to move the object to a new position, place the mouse pointer in the middle of the selected object and drag it to a new position.

If you draw several related objects, you can select all the objects at once and drag them together to a new location. Select the first object and then hold down the **Shift** key and select subsequent objects, as needed. When you drag any of the objects to a new location, all the selected objects move together.

At times you will want to delete a particular object from your document. Simply select the object and then press **Delete** to remove it.

You will find that the Drawing toolbar provides you with all the tools (except natural artistic ability) you need to create fairly sophisticated custom images. A little practice with the various tools goes a long way in helping you create objects that add interest to your documents.

INSERTING IMAGES FROM SCANNERS AND OTHER SOURCES

You can also place images into your Word documents that do not currently exist as a picture or clip art file. You can actually attach to a particular *input device*, such as a scanner or digital camera, and then have it scan an image or take a picture that is inserted into your document.

PLAIN ENGLISH

> **Input Device** Any device, such as a scanner or a digital camera, that can be attached to your computer and used to acquire a picture.

Word enables you to acquire images from an attached scanner, a digital camera, or other device such as a video camera. All you have to do is set up the device so that it works on your computer (consult your device's documentation), and Word can use it to capture any image that device provides.

To insert an image from an attached device, follow these steps:

1. Place the insertion point in the document where you want to insert the image.

2. Select the **Insert** menu, point at **Picture**, and then click **From Scanner or Camera**. The Insert Picture from Camera or Scanner dialog box appears.

3. Click the **Device** drop-down box and select the device you want to capture the picture from (this is necessary only if you have more than one device attached).

4. Click the **Insert** button. The device scans the image or, in the case of a camera, downloads a particular image and places the image in your document.

In this lesson, you learned how to insert pictures and clip art and create graphics. In the next lesson, you will learn how to set up a mail merge in Word.

LESSON 21
Working with Larger Documents

In this lesson, you learn how to work with larger documents, including inserting section breaks and building a table of contents.

ADDING SECTIONS TO DOCUMENTS

When you work with larger documents, you might have several parts in the document, such as a cover page, a table of contents, and the body of the document. In most cases, these different parts of the document require different formatting and layout attributes. To divide a document into different parts that have different layouts, use sections. A *section* is a defined portion of the document that can contain its own set of formatting options. You can divide a document into as many sections as you need.

TIP

> **Section**   A portion of a document (defined with marks that you insert) that can be formatted differently from the rest of the document or other distinct sections of the document.

When you first begin a new document, the document consists of one section with consistent page formatting throughout the document. If you look at the status bar in a new document, you find that it reads "Sec 1," which means that the insertion point is currently in Section 1 of the document (which would be the entire document, in this case).

Sections are defined in your document by section breaks (which means a certain position in the document serves as the break between the existing section and the new section you insert). To place additional section breaks in a document, follow these steps:

1. Place the insertion point where you would like to insert the new section break.

2. Select **Insert, Break**. The Break dialog box appears. In the lower half of the Break dialog box, several section break types are available (see Figure 21.1).

FIGURE 21.1
Select your type of section break in the Break dialog box.

- **Next Page**—A page break is placed in the document and the new section begins on this new page.

- **Continuous**—The new section starts at the insertion point and continues for the rest of the document (or until it comes to the next defined section).

- **Even Page**—The new section starts on the next even-numbered page.

- **Odd Page**—The new section starts on the next odd-numbered page.

3. Select the option button for the type of section break you want to place in the document.

4. Click **OK** to insert the new section into the document.

Your new section break appears in the document. In the Normal view, the section break appears as a double horizontal line marked with the text "Section Break" followed by the type of section you selected. If you are working in the Print Layout view, the only way to see which section you're in is to look at the number displayed on the status bar (see Figure 21.2).

Section breaks are visible in the Normal View.

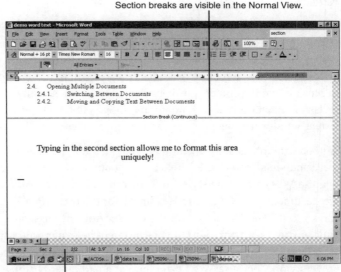

The status bar lists which section your pointer is in.

FIGURE 21.2
You can easily find out which section of a document you are in by reading the status bar or switching the document to Normal View.

After you have the new section in the document, you can apply page formatting to it as needed.

If you want to delete a section break, place the mouse pointer in the selection area and select the section break as you would any other line of text (this won't work in the Print Layout view). After the section break is selected, press the **Delete** key to remove it.

CREATING A TABLE OF CONTENTS

If you want to make it easy for the reader of a large document to find specific sections or parts of the document, you must include a table of contents. Creating a table of contents in Word relies heavily on using specific text styles to format and organize your document. As long as you do this, creating a table of contents is actually very straightforward.

For example, you can use either Word's built-in heading styles (Heading 1, Heading 2, Heading 3, and so forth) to format the different levels of headings in the document, or you can create your own styles to do so. Using these headings requires you to use methodology to break down the contents of your document, such as using section levels or chapter levels. The important thing is that you use them consistently to format the various headings in the document.

A good example is a document that is divided into parts and then further subdivided into chapters (each part contains several chapters). If you use Word's heading styles to format the different division levels in the document, you would use Heading 1 for the parts (Part I, Part II, and so forth) and Heading 2 for the chapter titles. By assigning these built-in styles (or your own) to your different headings, you can generate a table of contents that shows two levels: parts and chapters. This process works because Word can pinpoint a particular heading level by the style that you've assigned to it (for more about working with and creating styles, see Lesson 12, "Working with Styles").

After you've set your various headings for parts, chapters, or other divisions into your document and have assigned a particular style to each group of headings, you are ready to use the Word Table of Contents feature to generate the actual table of contents.

To create a table of contents using the Word heading styles—or unique styles that you have created—follow these steps:

1. Create a blank page at the beginning of your document for your table of contents (or create a new section in which to

place your table of contents) and place your insertion point in it.

2. On the **Insert** menu, choose **Reference, Index and Tables**.

3. When the Index and Tables dialog box appears, select the **Table of Contents** tab (see Figure 21.3).

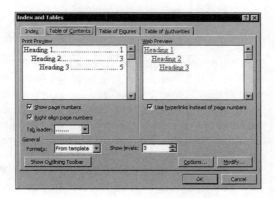

FIGURE 21.3
The Table of Contents tab on the Index and Tables dialog box is where you specify the options for your new table of contents. You see both a Print Preview and a Web Preview.

4. The Table of Contents tab provides you with a preview of the table of contents (TOC) hierarchy for Word's built-in heading styles. If you used the Word heading styles to format and specify the various division levels in your document, you can skip down to step 7. If you made your own unique heading or section styles, click the **Options** button.

5. The Table of Contents Options dialog box appears. This is where you specify the styles you used to format the various TOC levels in your document. Scroll down through the **Available Styles** list. To specify a style as a TOC hierarchical level, type the level number (1, 2, 3, and so on) into the appropriate style's TOC level box.

6. When you have selected the styles that serve as your various TOC levels, click **OK** to return to the Table of Contents tab.

7. To select a style for the TOC, click the **Formats** drop-down list. You can choose from several styles, such as Classic, Distinctive, and Fancy. After you select a format, a preview is provided in the Print Preview and Web Preview areas of the dialog box.

 TIP

> **Open the Outlining Toolbar for Quick Access of TOC Features**   If you will be editing headings in the document that will affect the TOC after you generate it, you might want to click the **Show Outlining Toolbar** button on the Table of Contents tab. This opens the Outlining toolbar. After generating the TOC and doing any editing in the document, you can use the Update TOC button on the Outlining toolbar to quickly regenerate the TOC. The toolbar also provides a Go to TOC button that can be used to quickly move from anywhere in the document back to the TOC.

8. Use the various check boxes on the tab to select or deselect options for formatting the table of contents. After you've specified options such as right align, page numbers, and the tab leader style, you are ready to generate the table of contents; click **OK**.

Your new table of contents appears in the document (see Figure 21.4). You can add a title to the table of contents and format the text as needed. If you want to remove the table of contents from the document, place the mouse pointer in the selection area to the left of the table of contents. Click to select the TOC. Press the **Delete** key to remove it from the document.

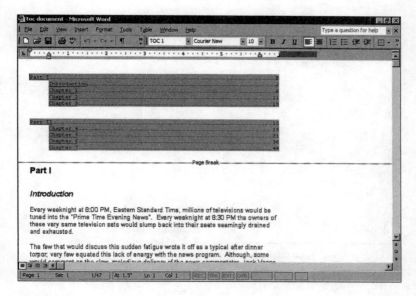

FIGURE 21.4
The table of contents is generated at the insertion point in your document. You can add your own title.

TIP

> **Use the TOC to Quickly Move to a Particular Chapter**   A
> real slick feature associated with the table of contents in
> your document is the ability to quickly jump to a partic-
> ular part of your document. For example, if you wanted
> to move to the beginning of Chapter 3 in the document
> from the TOC, press **Ctrl+click** on the Chapter 3 notation
> in the table of contents. You are linked directly to the
> beginning of Chapter 3.

In this lesson you learned how to insert sections into a document and
create a table of contents.

INDEX